Praise for How to Build a Multi-Level Money Machine

"Who else but Randy Gage would have the audacity to write *How to Build a Multi-Level Money Machine*—and then have the book actually show you how to do just that...? Only Randy could've pulled it off. A really great book from one of the few, true, card-carrying Masters of Network Marketing."

John Milton Fogg
Author, *The Greatest Networker in the World*

"Randy Gage is one of the very few masters of building a 'forever' network marketing organization. This simple yet powerful how-to book will show you the ways and the whys of building your own financial freedom with honor and integrity."

Richard Brooke
Chairman & CEO
Oxyfresh Worldwide Inc.

"A thorough step-by-step checklist that any new distributor or leader could follow. The list includes not only what to do—but why you should do it."

Tom 'Big Al' Schreiter
KAAS Publishing

"Can knock *years* off your learning curve as you strive for success in Network Marketing. Packed with valuable gems of info that—when applied—can propel your business into the very top of your company's pay plan at turbo speed. Who wants success at any other pace?"

Art Burleigh
30-Year MLM Veteran & Top Producer

"This is a must-have resource if you want to be successful in Network Marketing. We always recommend it to everyone on our team. No one walks their talk like Randy Gage."

Julie Mirr & Dr. Tim Berry
Diamond Directors
Agel Enterprises

"This book will help you transform your business. It is a must read."

Robert Butwin
Author, *Street Smart Networking*
Multi-Million Dollar MLM Income Earner

"Brilliant! A significant contribution to the science side of Network Marketing. Destined to be in the library of every serious student of Network Marketing."

Art Jonak
Founder, Network Marketing Mastermind Event

"Randy Gage's book, *How to Build a Multi-Level Money Machine*, is the MLM bible of our age. It took me to a whole new level of wealth building."

Mark Hammond
Sales Director
Mega Wealth Mentors, L.L.C.

"What I appreciate MOST about Randy's work is that he shares not 'what works' but 'what duplicates' and in Network Marketing, it is DUPLICATION that = SUCCESS!"

Kathy Schneider
Senior Director
Scent-Sations

"Anyone who has an interest in creating multiple income streams should run and get Randy's new book. We listened to Randy's advice and were able to create a $30,000 to $40,000 monthly cash flow in less than two years working 10 to 15 hours per week. Now more than ever our entire profession needs this valuable information on the power of time zone and people leverage."

Billy Looper & Wes Anderson
Double Diamond Directors
Agel Enterprises

"Everything you write or put in DVD is easy to understand and implement. You have provided me with a road map for MLM. Thank you."

Nancy Reagan
President
N. Reagan & Company, Inc.

"Been in the biz for 17 years full-time and the book makes sense because it helped me pull it all together. When my 19-year-old joined the biz, she read it and commented 'Oh, right! Let's get going!'"

Dawn Gough
Gold SED
Kleeneze

"An excellent step-by-step manual for both the newest person in the Network who hopes to build a profitable business, as well as for the experienced networker who is looking to fine-tune their skills and become wildly successful! I have learned many skills from Randy's book that I have been able to take directly to my team to help them become successful, and in return, has launched me to the top of the pay plan. Get this book into the hands of your leaders and watch your business explode!"

Sue Mazza
Senior Executive Unit Leader
Avon Products

"This is by far the best MLM tutorial I have ever seen. From finishing the book and to the next month, my personal and group turnover increased by 125%. It made me see how to systematically work the business, simple and without any fuzz. This is a MUST READ for any networker with leadership ambitions!"

Michael Holm
LR Health & Beauty Systems

"This is the best book in the industry. It has all the 'how tos' as well as the philosophies you need to build a big business."

Chris Hughes
Platinum Executive Director &
Millionaire Club Member
Pre-Paid Legal

"*How to Build a Multi-Level Money Machine* was the breakthrough for me in my business. From Randy I learned the fundamentals I needed, how to create a system that could be followed many levels deep, without my being a part of the equation. I finally achieved true duplication throughout my organization. This is one book every business builder must have in their library."

Stephanie Sterling
Senior Director
Scent-Sations

"I recommend this book to all serious networkers. It is about what we really go through in our business, no BS...direct info that we really need to grow big in our network business."

Jean-Francois Viau
Millionaire Club
Immunotec

"I believe it's one of the best books on Network Marketing I have ever read. I have recommended this book to a lot of distributors in my network and I have seen that everyone has learned a lot from this book."

Pranaya Bahl
1st
Amway India Enterprises

"After reading *How to Build a Multi-Level Money Machine*, I became fully aware of how to create duplication, utilize my company's tools, and work with the leaders in my group! Randy Gage is a master of MLM and has been an incredible mentor to me, even though we are in different companies!!"

Matt Borden
Presidents Club TC
ACN

"If you have a desire to turn your dreams into reality, you need to have this book in your library, apply the principles in it, and refer to it often."

Dennis Williams
Royal Ambassador
Nikken

"Thank you very much, Randy. Your life experience has changed and upgraded my orientation in how to build a lucrative and successful Network Marketing in Bali, Indonesia. *How To Build a Multi-Level Money Machine* is my Marketing Bible."

Dominikus Uja
Level 7
PT. Wootekh Indonesia

"This book always gives me the confidence to move forward and is my companion whenever things don't fall to my expectations. That's why I also bought a few copies of the book and gave it to my leaders."

Edwin Q. Mamaril
Executive Senior Star Diamond
DXN International

"Thanks to the great book *How to build a Multi-Level Money Machine*, I was inspired and I've reached a higher pin rank. Now, thanks to these tactics described in the book, I'm strongly on my way to reaching the next level before next summer!"

Guy Janssens
GET
Herbalife

"The book helped me learn how to build a system. I knew how to recruit; however, I did not know how to keep the people I recruited. I did not realize I was reading Volume #2. Can't wait for the new book. Randy Gage for life."

Cedric Carr
Diamond
Ardyss International

"I have worked in the training/recruiting business for the last 15 years of my career and when it comes to being a Professional Network Marketer, Randy takes you from the basic fundamentals and practices to the entrepreneur mentality to be successful not only in the business, but also in life. A must read for any person who is really serious in taking this profession to a prominent level in their life!"

Jorge Melendez
Senior Director
Alternative Music Promotions

"There's no one better to show you the skills, the how-tos (and how-*not*-tos), the essential ingredients of success in this business than Randy Gage. I've been watching and learning from him for years; the breadth and depth of his grasp of MLM—and his ability to articulate and teach it—never ceases to amaze me."

John David Mann
Coauthor, *The Go-Giver*

How To Build A Multi-Level Money Machine

The Science of Network Marketing

Randy Gage

Published by Prime Concepts Group, Inc.
7570 W. 21st Street N., Suite 1038A
Wichita, KS 67205 USA
Toll-Free: 1-800-946-7804
Local: (316) 942-1111
www.RandyGage.com
www.NetworkMarketingTimes.com

Printed in the United States of America

Library of Congress Cataloging-in-Publication Data
Gage, Randy.
    How to build a multi-level money machine : the
    science of network marketing / Randy Gage. — 4th ed.
        p. cm.
        LCCN: 2001088973
        ISBN: 978-0-9673164-6-8

        1. Multilevel marketing.   I. Title.

    HF5415.126.G34 2001   658.8'4
                                 QBI01-200369

Dedication

This book is dedicated to those who still dare to dream. Without you, this business wouldn't exist, and millions would have lost the hope, dignity, and freedom it provides. Never forget that what you do matters. A lot.

Table of Contents

Acknowledgments

I'm blessed to be living a dream life, thanks to Network Marketing. I can do that because of the tireless work of others who have supported, nurtured, and developed the profession over the years. **John Milton Fogg** and **John David Mann** started *Upline* magazine back in the day and did as much as anyone to give Network Marketing credibility. **Mark Yarnell** picked up the torch and spread the message in *SUCCESS* magazine. **Tom Schreiter** has been championing the profession for more than 20 years. **Len Clements** has stood up for keeping it real. More recently **Chris and Josephine Gross** and their team at *Networking Times* and **George Madiou** and his team at *The Network Marketing Magazine* have continued the job. As we move into the future, **Art Jonak** and another generation of Jedi Knights are leading the tribe. Thank you all.

Introduction to the 4th Edition

As I went through this book revisiting what I had written in earlier editions, it was interesting to note what had changed—and what had remained the same.

Predictably, the general principles on which the business is built hadn't changed a bit. They are timeless.

Some approaches in the marketing arena have evolved and some have been completely revamped.

Technology and the Internet have reached mass acceptance and can now play a bigger role in recruiting, training, and communication. The advent of Web 2.0 and the social media sites have dramatically influenced the ability to expand a warm market. So, you'll see that information greatly expanded and updated.

I factored in the current economic challenges the world faces and included much of the material from *The MLM Revolution*, my manifesto on what's right and what's wrong with our profession.

The other big change you'll notice is in the recruiting process. I no longer am recommending one-on-one or two-on-one presentations as part of your prospecting pipeline. You'll see a much stronger emphasis on using third-party tools. This is to reduce the learning time for new distributors and increase long-term duplication, based on the extraordinary results I've generated with this approach over the last several years.

Two other factors come into play in the equation—each at odds with the other, however...

First is the broad-based acceptance and credibility Network Marketing has developed in the mass consciousness. We boast companies with billion-dollar-plus revenues, are publicly traded, and have even created some media darlings. Virtually everyone today now knows someone earning a large income in Network Marketing. And the mainstream financial media, venture capitalists, and general public have gone from being scornful or skeptical about our business to being quite intrigued.

That's the good news. On the other side of the equation has been the explosion of marketing messages assaulting all of us at every opportunity. We are bombarded by ads on Web sites, on public transportation, on your place mat, even in public bathrooms. This onslaught of saturation advertising has left prospects shell-shocked and more defensive than ever.

Yet never has the world needed what we have to offer more...

Thus, in the swirl of all these convergent forces, I have tried to guide you through the best practices that are working in the space right now. This revised, fourth edition is my take on how you can deal effectively with the challenges we face today, allowing you to create the success you are seeking and manifest your dream life.

Like the earlier editions, this book offers no abstract theories or suggested experiments. What you'll find between these pages is the real-world system I have developed over 20 years and used personally to create a huge worldwide network of distributors that has produced literally billions of dollars in sales for my team and my protégés.

What this book can do for you...

Building upon my success, you can cut many years

off your growth curve and develop your own network much faster than you've ever been able to before. You'll learn what attracts prospects to you and how to present to them effectively. You'll discover the kind of people you want to sponsor, and whom you would be better to screen out in the early stages of the process.

Once you're well educated in the sponsoring process, you will learn how to manage—and keep growing—a large network.

You'll find out how to spend your time, how to develop leaders, and how to counsel them. Most importantly, you'll learn how to empower those leaders to develop new ones. By the time you're done, you will have a clear understanding of a fundamental, profound truth about Network Marketing:

You don't grow your network. You grow your people—and they grow your group.

You will find I'm not big on motivational clichés and "rah-rah" platitudes. I believe that if you can show people specifically how they can accomplish a desired goal—they will motivate themselves.

By the time you've finished the book, you will:

- Have a realistic view of how wealth is created in the business;
- Know the key components for developing true duplication;
- Understand what top income earners do to build effectively; and,
- Have a specific game plan for making that happen.

My hope is that you'll view Network Marketing as the professional career it has become and will lock arms with me to continue raising the standards of this empowering business.

Unlike the corporate world—with its downsizing and rat-eat-rat competition—Network Marketing offers you the opportunity to nurture and empower the inherent talents in all those you sponsor. In this business, success means the chance to develop spiritually, intellectually, emotionally, and financially while you contribute in a positive way to others.

What you won't find in this book are canned scripts, closing techniques, or manipulative sales strategies. While there are many who teach these methods in our business, they don't produce real duplication, and thus can't provide true success. At its very core, Network Marketing is a teaching business, and this book is dedicated to teaching you how to teach your own people.

As you undertake this journey of challenge, adventure, and growth, you will attract others who share your vision and follow your example. You will lead them for a short time, then release them as they unfold into leaders and start the process all over again. You will feel pride, joy, and a sense of accomplishment few ever experience. You will know that what you do means something—and that your community is a little bit better place because you have contributed.

Building a large, exponentially growing network is not easy—it's not supposed to be. It is simple, however. If you are open to being coached, follow the system, and don't give up at the first sign of challenge, you can achieve abundant and lasting success in Network Marketing.

This book is generic, so you can recommend it freely to your entire team to produce faster recruiting and stronger duplication. I suggest you read through it in its entirety first. Then revisit particular chapters as needed to refresh your memory or increase your skill level in a particular area.

Please think of me as your surrogate sponsor, here to assist your regular sponsor in helping you live your dreams in this amazing business of Network Marketing.

You can stay in touch with the latest developments by following the MLM Success Blog and signing up for my MLM Leadership Report, both at NetworkMarketingTimes.com. I'm committed to helping you reach success!

Randy Gage
February, 2009
Key West, Florida

How To Build A Multi-Level Money Machine

Chapter One:

The Red Pill or the Blue Pill?

Maybe it happened when governments around the world began taking the taxes they coerced from their citizens and used them to prop up mismanaged Wall Street brokers, insurance companies, car manufacturers, and other private businesses. It might have been when people realized the banking system itself was bankrupt.

Perhaps it clicked when the airline executives could segue into bankruptcy and then segue out after slashing their pension plan obligations. Or maybe it took place with the steady revelations of company after company, cooking their books to rip off investors and workers while enriching their crooked executives.

One thing is certain...

Around the world, people began to wake up, snap out of their corporate comas, and think again. They began to question the morality of the standard business model, rethink their priorities, and wonder if their governments really could provide for their golden years.

The really savvy people went yet further, deciding that they alone could provide for their financial future, and they could never again leave it to chance from employers or governments.

Even more, they decided that work should have

meaning, that what they do for a living should offer hope and help, and that principles matter.

In the midst of the most severe economic downturn in decades, they began to dream again...

They rediscovered the dreams they had dreamt as a child—and realized they didn't have to give them up just because they lived in the grown-up world now.

They asked themselves what their dream job would look like. And the answers that came back were not:

- Shift supervisor at Burger King;
- Bureaucrat at the driver's license agency;
- Line foreman at the auto assembly plant;
- Mid-level manager in a large corporation; or,
- Clerk in the insurance field.

Not exactly shocking. But what was perhaps really surprising was that the answer to the perfect job question did not come back as being a:

- Doctor, attorney, or accountant;
- Corporate VP or executive; or,
- Traditional business owner.

Because, for once, people (at least some of them) stopped thinking about a dream job and started thinking about a DREAM LIFE—knowing that, in reality, the two are inseparable.

The People Who Get This...

You can make a fortune, but if you have to sacrifice your kids, relationships, or health for it, what's the point? You can afford lots of things, but where's the joy if there is no one to enjoy them with? When is the last time you saw a hearse pulling a U-Haul trailer behind it?

There is a select and growing group of people who really get this...

Others discovered that going through the motions of a monotonous job, simply because it requires only 40 hours a week, is not going to bring true happiness either. They understand that the drudgery of work with no meaning doesn't open the doorway to satisfaction in the free time they have left. So this group gets it too.

So who are these people that understand the new reality of today's world?

They come from many occupations and backgrounds and all age groups. Some are Mensa members, some are high school dropouts; some are both.

Many have sought refuge from the deceit, politics, and soul-killing inertia of the corporate world. Others have fled the mediocrity of blue-collar labor, seeking to add some adventure to their lives. Still others were entrepreneurs who woke up one morning (or couldn't sleep one night), and realized they didn't own their businesses—their businesses owned them.

If you ask the people in this select group what a dream life looks like, they will tell you it is a mélange of work and recreation, contribution and challenge, spiritual reflection and intellectual stimulation.

The MLM Revolution...

This group of people found their way to Network Marketing (sometimes called Multi-Level Marketing or MLM for short). But you won't find us wearing corny buttons, accosting people on the street corner, or driving

3

around with magnetic signs on our automobiles.

We didn't join an industry; we joined a profession. And we didn't do it just to get rich. (Although many of us, myself included, initially showed up seeking wealth.) The people who become network marketing professionals appreciate the wealth we can create, but as we understand more about the business, our consciousness expands to a much bigger picture.

Yes, they will tell you that prosperity is important to happiness. But they aren't the type to sit on the sofa watching *The Secret* 47 times, wondering when their Lamborghini is going to roar up into their driveway by itself.

And they have a broader view of prosperity than most. You will never hear them utter statements like "It's just money" or "They're only things," because they know that money and material things are the lubrication of life. They realize it's pretty hard to feel prosperous if you can't pay the rent, make your car payment, or buy groceries for your family.

But they don't make the mistake many do by thinking that prosperity is about only money either. They know that true prosperity includes good health, loving relationships, and a spiritual side to life. When they speak of living a life of abundance, they mean doing so in all areas.

The real draw for most of the people in this group is the ultimate product they sell: Freedom. The freedom from lack, the freedom to really live a life of meaning, significance, and abundance—in color, out loud, and BIG.

Complete History of the Universe...
(Abridged Edition)

Network Marketing began in 1956 when Dr. Forest Shaklee started the Shaklee Corporation and Rich DeVos and Jay Van Andel began what later morphed into the Amway Corporation.

The first distributors in these programs were definitely skewed towards the selling model, with a much smaller focus on recruitment and the override commissions that could be generated. Early Shaklee and Amway stars were the ones that sold the most vitamins or soap.

In the seventies these companies (and many others that had started in the business) began to attract more professional people, and they were intrigued by the possibilities and potential of the leverage that could be produced by duplication and recruiting. This put the MLM business on the radar and instigated some more attention from regulators. Making matters worse, the large incomes being produced by legitimate network marketers was being noticed by people with not-so-honorable intentions. So at this time, there was an explosion of chain letters, Ponzi schemes, and illegal pyramids attempting to pass themselves off as legitimate MLM opportunities.

At the same time, the old model of product distribution was facing serious challenges. The business model—ship something from Europe to the U.S. by boat, where it was sent across the country to a wholesaler, who trucked it to a rack jobber, who sold it to a retail outlet, that stored it in a warehouse, and then moved it to a store, where the consumer could finally purchase it—began to break down.

Network marketing companies recognized the new world of commerce and prospered...

A company could manufacture a product and ship it direct to its distributors, without all of the inefficient parasites in the middle. These distributors consumed the products themselves and used conversational viral marketing to spread the word among their friends and acquaintances.

Although it faced some attacks from the media and later government regulators, Network Marketing—and its sister companies in the Direct Selling arena—continued to develop and now does well in excess of US$120 billion a year in sales around the world. It has gained tremendous acceptance globally, being featured in mainstream business and financial publications such as *SUCCESS, Forbes, Fortune,* and *USA Today.*

The new reality...

In every group of people, a few will retire young, rich, and worry-free. A few more will work hard and long but finally retire in security if not comfort. Most, however, will slog through 45 or 50 years of their life in the rat race, only to eke out a living in their "golden years" on a meager pension.

What separates these groups? What are the secrets possessed by those in the first one? And more importantly, how do you make sure you wind up in the first group?

I'm not referring to captains of industry, the market traders, or the real estate tycoons. For while many of these people have amassed great monetary wealth, they don't retire early, and they certainly do not appear to be worry-free. In fact, it's quite the opposite. They're winning the rat race—but they're often living like rats.

Put the lime in the coconut...

The group I'm talking about is the next generation of entrepreneurs—the people who have built "drink out of a coconut" incomes. They've created multi-level money machines that shower them with rewards, whether they remain working or choose to spend their days on a tropical beach, with their toes in the sand, sipping from that coconut. They are the new breed of network marketing professionals.

The parallels of how these people reached this success are intriguing indeed...

You might think they attained their status through higher education, but this is not necessarily the case. Many members of this group are high school dropouts (like myself), and we all know that many people with multiple university degrees make their living driving taxis.

And while the people in my group worked hard to attain their considerable prosperity, that alone was not the deciding factor. In fact, although I'm slightly embarrassed to admit this, most people work harder than I do, but they certainly don't receive the rewards I do.

The mechanic who services my cars, the man who landscapes my lawn, my massage therapist, and my usual waitress at my favorite restaurant all work much harder than I do. Yet none of them are wealthy doing what they do. In fact, they work a lot harder for a lot less. Not one of them shows even a remote chance of retiring early. So we can't say that hard work alone creates prosperity. These people, and millions more like them, are prisoners in the Matrix—a broken economic model.

They are trapped in the trading-time-for-money trap.

They bought into herd thinking and became worker drones in the collective. To receive more money, they must work harder and longer. Most are stuck in salaried positions or jobs restricting overtime, so one job doesn't even offer them the opportunity to trade more time for more money. As a result, they put their spouse or partner to work, which of course is still not enough.

So they take a second job. And sometimes, so does their spouse. The result is three- and four-income families—desperately trying to trade more time for more money. Then no one's raising the kids. They learn about life from playing video games. They need their parents desperately, but Mom and Dad are out working, trying to provide a good life for their children. It's a vicious cycle.

And a very foolish one. Because as long as you play the trading-time–for-money game, you can never reach true financial security.

The people in my group have discovered that attaining true economic freedom requires that you employ two basic prosperity principles:

1) You must employ the concept of leverage to escape the trading-time-for-money dilemma; and

2) You must be able to look in the mirror every

morning and know you're talking to the boss. You must forgo the structure of being someone's employee and embrace becoming an entrepreneur.

Once you're willing to take these steps, manifesting prosperity is no longer a wild pipe dream, but something you can really accomplish.

When you take the entrepreneurial excitement of working for yourself and combine that with leveraging yourself through a network of other excited entrepreneurs—the results are exponentially spectacular. The synergistic process creates a whole that is much more powerful than its individual parts. Done properly, *the end result of building your network is a self-perpetuating, multi-level money machine.*

And you can own it.

Network Marketing is one of the new models for creating wealth today. It's practiced in more than one hundred countries and territories around the globe. Millions of independent distributors produce an annual volume estimated at more than US$120 billion.

Cool Biz...

Why should you get involved with Network Marketing? There are probably as many answers as there are distributors. Usually, though, it comes down to the kind of lifestyle networking can give you. Some of the unique benefits of this business include:

- Choosing the people you work with;
- Going into business with a small investment;
- Working from home;

- Picking the hours you work;
- Discovering unique products not available elsewhere;
- Getting lucrative tax advantages;
- Enjoying the opportunity for an unlimited income; and,
- Having the chance to build your success while empowering others to succeed.

You can sum it up as freedom from the rat race. These benefits are just not available anywhere else. While most people realize they won't get these benefits working *for* someone, a lot of them mistakenly believe that having their own traditional business will provide these benefits.

Not likely.

As a former Chamber of Commerce president and owner of ten small and medium-sized businesses, I can personally attest that, in many ways, owning a traditional business can be more limiting than working for somebody. Because of things like employee turnover, inventories, large investments, personal guarantees, government regulation, and market competition, you often work longer hours for less money than you pay your employees. You don't really own a small business—the small business owns you.

People today are fed up with out-of-balance work situations that rob them of their family life. And they're tired of merger mania, leveraged buy-outs, and layoffs. Today they're looking for work with significance, lifestyle rewards, and quality time with their loved ones. Which is exactly where Network Marketing comes in...

Because, unlike the corporate rat race, in Network Marketing you never get ahead by holding others back. The road to success in Network Marketing is traveled by *empowering* others. In fact, the more people you help reach success, the more successful you will become.

If you're looking to get rich quick, Network Marketing is really not for you. However, if you're willing to work hard on a part-time basis for two to four years—you really can build a lifetime of financial freedom.

The flexible hours make it a perfect business to start while you keep your current job, even if you're a student or a housewife with children. You can also start the business with a very small investment, usually in the neighborhood of between US$500 to $1,500 to begin.

Network Marketing has emerged as the last real chance in the free enterprise system for the average person without large capital to become financially free.

Once you decide to work in this exciting profession, you're in for a career of unlimited financial opportunity, and the chance to make a meaningful difference in the lives of the people you care most about.

So do you have what it takes to succeed in the business? We'll find out next!

Chapter Two:

The Secrets of MLM Success

N etwork Marketing has produced some of the most amazing success stories in the world. Virtually every company has its "rags to riches" stories of everyday people who went from poor or modest beginnings to earning more money in a month than most people bring down in a year.

From the couple living in their in-laws' garage to a bankrupt minister in Texas, from the single mother on welfare to the young man in Taiwan who rode his bicycle to opportunity meetings—these people and thousands more like them have their unique stories to tell.

Yet, across the business, you will find striking similarities in the ultra-successful people in all companies. These common traits are the prerequisites for long-term success in the business.

Everyone in the group is a dreamer. They stopped buying the gloom and doom of the masses and reconnected to the vision of greatness we all once had for ourselves.

If Morpheus were to offer them the red pill or the blue pill, they would always choose the trip down the rabbit hole rather than the safety of the Matrix— because they know that in the new reality, the safe choice is where the real risk is. They know that those who choose being "safe" become the worker drones in the collective. The people who are willing to take what the herd would perceive as risks are the ones who reap the reward of a life worth living. Bold is the new safe.

Everyone in the group is a critical thinker. They reject herd thinking and practice discernment. They are curious by nature and open to challenging their most deeply held foundational beliefs. They are not cynics, but they *are* skeptical of conventional wisdom, they question authority, and they want to know the reasoning behind a premise. They know that any beliefs they have that serve them will survive a healthy skepticism, and any beliefs that don't stand up under scrutiny need to be replaced.

Everyone in this group is a worker. They don't look for the free lunches and get-rich schemes. Far from running away from work, they wake up, throw the sheets off the bed, and actually look forward to work! Being a network marketing professional means welcoming challenge, growth, and adventure and helping others while helping oneself. So they love what they do, and don't need a weekend, a six-pack, and ten DVDs to escape from their "job." They have discovered how to balance work and life and bring meaning to both.

Everyone in this group is a good teacher. They recognize that real duplication comes from their possessing good teaching skills much more than selling skills. They follow a formula that allows large numbers of people to replicate their actions.

Everyone is this group is also a student. They have a passion for lifelong learning and set aside daily time for quiet reflection and self-development. It's important that you continually sharpen your saw. Books, DVDs, CDs, or online seminars—the medium is not important.

What matters is that you dedicate yourself to always being a little better today than you were yesterday.

Initially, my biggest mistake in the business was thinking that success would come from changing others. I soon learned that success would come from changing myself. The actions you take and the examples you set create a ripple effect that impacts everything around you in a positive way. To change the world, you must first change yourself.

Everyone in this group is a leader. They weren't born a leader. Nobody appointed them to the position, and they couldn't care less about titles, hierarchy, or conformity. They are called to lead from the small, still voice in their soul.

They lead because they have belief. Belief in a better way, belief in contributing to others, and a belief that prosperity is everyone's birthright. And they know that conviction comes with a responsibility to share that belief with the larger community.

The rules of the corporate world don't apply in Network Marketing. In this business, you get ahead not by beating out other people or holding them down, but by helping them to grow. The more people you make successful, the more successful you become.

A corporation has room for one president, a few vice presidents, more middle managers, and lots of low-level jobs. In Network Marketing, you encourage everyone to reach for the higher levels of success. There is no limit to the number of people who can reach the top of your compensation plan.

If you approach the business with an attitude that focuses on what you are going to make off those whom you sponsor, they will receive those signals and you will face many challenges. Focus instead on how you can help others, and your own success will naturally come about.

Chapter Three:

Choosing the Right Company for You

Because the money involved in Network Marketing is so lucrative, the industry has attracted its share of bottom feeders and scam artists. Buyers clubs, chain letters, and illegal pyramids do everything they can to position themselves as though they are legitimate network marketing companies.

It's important that you understand the difference between the legitimate network marketing business model versus the illegal schemes. There is even confusion among some government regulators on this distinction, so let's sketch out what separates the two.

As a practical matter, it's impossible for regulators to predict and legislate all of the infinite variations of legal and illegal marketing programs. For that reason, multi-level and anti-pyramid laws are drafted and interpreted very broadly. This allows regulators to encompass all of the possible variations of illegal schemes and have a jurisdictional basis to close them down.

For now, let's look at the two major distinctions used by knowledgeable experts to determine if a program is a legitimate multi-level opportunity:

The first focus is the conceptual design of the compensation plan. More specifically, does it compensate participants merely for introducing others to the program or for the sales of goods or services to the end consumer?

If the plan focuses on rewarding participants for recruiting—it is a pyramid. If the commission structure is geared on product/service sales to the end consumer—it passes the first phase of the test.

The second analysis is on *the actual operation of the program*. Regardless of how the compensation plan is designed, regulators look at what the distributors actually spend their time doing. If the emphasis of the program is on recruiting rather than product or service sales, it can still be determined to be a pyramid.

And here is where advances in customer service have clouded the issue, confusing some regulators. Back in the day, you had to drive around town with a magnetic sign on your car and deliver products to all of your customers or you "played store" with a huge inventory set up in your home for customers to drop by. That is no longer necessary.

Companies have developed preferred customer and autoship programs, so independent distributors no longer have to handle product fulfillment, collections, sales tax, and other functions. They can simply enroll a customer into one of these programs and receive their retail profits. And many savvy customers sign up as distributors themselves in order to purchase their product wholesale. So you can spend a lot more time on recruiting and a lot less time on servicing customers. Some regulators haven't caught up to this new reality.

Here in the U.S., only a few sophisticated states have statutes that specifically define and regulate Multi-Level Marketing. Most states do have anti-pyramid laws. There are no comprehensive, defining laws on the national level here, nor in many other countries.

In the States, federal regulation comes primarily from administrative and judicial decisions that are the result of lawsuits from private parties and the Federal Trade Commission (FTC).

Piecing together these decisions along with the definitions created by the state legislators gives you the main elements that define a Multi-Level Marketing program. From an anti-pyramid standpoint, the most important determination in state statutes is whether the money participants earn is contingent upon recruiting others into the program. Thus, pyramids, endless chain schemes, and chain letters are illegal.

From a federal standpoint, the determination level is slightly different. While Canada has passed national anti-pyramid legislation, most countries have not. This is changing, however. Many central European and other countries have been victimized recently by large-scale pyramid schemes, a trend that is causing many nations to adopt legislation.

Here in the U.S., where Network Marketing began, there has still been no anti-pyramid statute passed by Congress. Most network marketing companies have developed their programs based upon the case law of Federal Court decisions and, more frequently, the decisions of the FTC.

The most cited decision used to define pyramid schemes is the FTC's 1975 ruling *In the Matter of Koscot Interplanetary, Inc.*[1] In that decision, the FTC held that "entrepreneurial chains" are characterized by "the payment by participants of money to the company in return for which they [the participants] receive (1) the right to sell a product, and (2) the right to receive in return for recruiting other participants into the program rewards which are *unrelated* to sale of the product to ultimate users."

The key here is the words "rewards which are *unrelated* to sale of the product to ultimate users"— meaning that you make money from things other than selling products personally or overrides on products sold by your people. If you're making money for these other things, such as signing up recruits or selling sales aids, there's a good chance you'll be determined to be illegal.

Because a company complies with the literal terms of the law does not guarantee that it will overcome all legal challenges. Because states and provinces have different legislation, a program may be legal in one state and found to be a pyramid in another. In addition, judges may interpret a statute in a matter not consistent with its literal terms.

And many underpaid government regulators are quite uneducated in this area and are not up to speed on relevant case law. In fact, it would appear that some of these regulators (and in some cases, judges) have never read the Constitution. A perfect case in point was *Capone vs. Nu Skin:*

First, the background...

This was a class action lawsuit initiated on behalf of Nu Skin's Canadian distributors. Nu Skin filed for a summary judgment from the court. (In this case, the U.S. District Court for the District of Utah.) In March of 1997, the court's Memorandum decision held that a Nu Skin distributorship might constitute a security.

Nu Skin, of course, maintained that this was ridiculous, since the entire investment involved purchasing a $60 distributor kit. The court, however, agreed with Ms. Capone that in order to "meaningfully participate in the Nu Skin marketing plan, it is necessary to purchase products every month to meet the personal volume and group volume requirements."

The court justified this by claiming "... a key feature of the Nu Skin Canada Marketing plan is that **every distributor**, in order to receive commissions from downline distributors, **must purchase 100 'points'** (equivalent to approximately $100.00 [U.S.]) worth of Nu Skin products. Similarly, distributors who become 'Executives' must account for $3,000 worth of product **purchases** every month among their distributors to be eligible for commission. Moreover, there is **evidence which suggests that commissions are paid regardless of whether the distributors actually retail the products they purchase.**"

Of course, there are two problems with this convoluted logic. First is the fact that distributors are not required to purchase products but rather to *produce volume*. It is certainly not unreasonable for Nu Skin or any other company to expect a distributor to produce a certain amount of personal volume to get paid overrides. In this case it was approximately $100. And distributors do not have to purchase it themselves. They can certainly market that much to their friends, relatives, or other customers, which obviously many do.

The second problem is the court suggesting that commissions, rebates, or overrides should be paid only on products that are retailed and not on those purchased by distributors who are their own best customer. There is absolutely no basis in law for this—it's simply a case of uneducated jurists trying to create new law.

Furthermore, the court went on to maintain that Nu Skin was a security because distributors could make "big money from building a sales force, becoming financially independent and the like." The court went on to state that the "promise of lucrative rewards for recruiting others tends to induce participants to focus on the recruitment side of the business at the expense of their retail marketing efforts, making it unlikely that meaningful opportunities for retail sales will occur."

In simpler terms, the court maintained that any program that potentially pays a distributor more from his group overrides than he makes retailing product personally satisfies the elements of an investment contract—and is then a security. Of course, this is ludicrous. If we followed this line of thinking to its logical conclusion, then the enterprising teenager who employed three or four other kids to shovel snow for the neighbors would be running a securities business as well.

At the risk of overstating the obvious—the courts sometimes forget that they are not supposed to make law but interpret it. Not only are courts making law, but it's bad law too. Lone federal judges are creating legislation faster than any congress or legislature. Several decisions, such as this one, clearly show the complete lack of understanding the courts have of MLM case law—and even the Constitution. Other countries face similar issues.

While this Nu Skin case is obviously an overreach

of government power, for the most part, regulators are honest, hardworking people simply protecting the public from unscrupulous schemes. Ultimately, the regulators will look to substance over form. Even if a program uses all the correct buzz words in its marketing materials—but does not enforce those policies that protect the public—the program will be treated just like one that does not have safeguards built in.

When it's all said and done, there are many inconsistencies among local and federal laws in the US—and among the other countries. Ultimately, there are three major factors that most regulators look to when trying to determine whether an operation is a pyramid or a legitimate network marketing program. And while these criteria are not necessarily embodied in a comprehensive statute, they are generally used because complying with these three criteria does protect the public from the dangers posed by pyramids. Let's look at them:

1) Substantial sales of products or services to ultimate users

The key here is that the products are reaching the end consumers. If someone asks you to buy $50,000 worth of water filters to qualify for a bonus or rank advancement, it's obvious you're not going to be the end user of all those. You've been front-loaded and this is not a legitimate program.

When product is getting to the end consumer—even if a large percentage of these consumers are distributors—this does meet the spirit and literal requirements of the law. Don't be confused by the one or two misguided decisions holding that distributor usage does not qualify as products to the ultimate consumer. As I mentioned earlier, many smart consumers today sign up as distributors so they can order direct and get a wholesale price. Or they start as distributors and decide the business is not for them but continue to purchase the product wholesale for years to come.

2) Commissions paid only on product usage, not headhunter fees

Your income must come as bonuses and overrides based on the volume produced by your organization. If you're paid simply for signing up someone or selling training materials—then you're probably in a pyramid.

A perfect example here is a "be a travel agent" type of deal that's all the rage as I write this edition.
These pseudo travel agents are facing serious legal challenges and getting a great deal of negative publicity. They're playing the aggrieved party and acting like they are being unfairly prosecuted.

But if you look at the actual annual report they publish, you can see that most of their sales—and most of the commissions paid out to their distributors—come from selling their marketing websites to the distributors themselves, not actually selling travel. This "mining the miners" rap is one of the biggest challenges in perception we legitimate network marketers face right now.

3) Inventory Repurchase Requirements

Most of the states with actual multi-level marketing laws require companies to repurchase inventory that is returned by their distributors. These states also require this policy to be stated in the distributor agreement.

In most cases, this buy-back requirement becomes effective only when the distributor terminates his or her distributorship. In other states, the company must repurchase any returned inventory simply if the distributor was unable to resell it within 90 days from buying it. (In both cases, there are some specifics. Usually, the buy-back is for 90 percent of the purchase price; the products must be resalable; and any commissions paid on the sold products may be deducted.)

Companies that comply with these three criteria are in line with both the letter and the spirit of the law.

Another area I need to address is the so-called "gifting" clubs. Their whole argument is that they don't need products, because the participants in the program voluntarily give "gifts" of money to the sponsorship line. Gifting programs are nothing more than knockoffs of chain letters, and we legitimate network marketers need to come down on them hard.

And how many times will people keep trying to bring back the discount clubs, which tout products or services that are of questionable value? These have been tried again and again and never worked yet. The marketplace doesn't support them, and regulators slam them because the discounts they promote are no more valuable than those available to anyone who simply shops around or is a member of organizations like AAA and AARP.

The product or service must be a legitimate one that people would buy at the retail price on the open market. (If no one would likely buy the product or service without participating in the compensation plan, you are probably looking at a pyramid.)

If you are counting on the lure of the business opportunity to so excite your prospect that he will not notice he is overpaying for your product, you will be greatly disappointed. A strong retail base of happy customers (who are not in it for the bonus checks) is one of the best indicators of a strong company.

Another option to beware of is the so-called Buyer's Clubs. These programs advertise "no selling required" and stress signing up everyone to buy wholesale. Many governments take a very dim view of such closed marketing systems, considering them pyramids. Here's why:

You can start a wholesale buyers club, just like Sam Walton did, and it's perfectly legal. But take a wholesale club and put a multi-level commission structure on it, and it becomes illegal in most cases, because it's a closed system paying commissions, with no option for retailing. Since everyone is a member, there's no one to sell to. If all we had to do was shop to earn, everybody would be doing it. But it's not that simple.

But it's not rocket science either...

It's not that hard to know what's right and what's wrong. At the end of the day, you should be able to take the compensation plan out of the equation. If the actual product or service provides a value equal to or greater than the price charged, you have something to work with. If you were not in the pay structure and you wouldn't be buying that product at that price anyway, you should probably steer clear of that program.

There is no compensation plan and no amount of hype that can sustain a company long-term with overpriced or substandard products. This doesn't mean your products must be cheaper than what's available elsewhere—just that they must be of an exceptional enough value that people still want them and are willing to pay for them.

This is not to say that your distributors won't be much better customers than non-distributors. They will. You will find that distributors have much higher volumes. They understand that anytime they buy a "Brand X" product, they are taking money out of their own pocket. Hence, they always make sure they have an adequate inventory so they never run out of product.

You'll also find they use the products more liberally because they're better educated about them, they find it easy to order the products, and they appreciate the savings of buying wholesale.

There's another big factor that figures in here...

Compliance. Especially if you're in a program with product lines such as skin care, nutrition, or weight management. Because distributors have a vested financial interest in the results, they are much more likely to follow the proper use guidelines, exercise, or make other necessary lifestyle changes that produce better product results. So distributors are much better customers, buy more, and are more loyal.

The lawyer stuff...

Because I'm not an attorney, none of the preceding

information is meant to be legal advice. Please use a lawyer for specific legal matters. What I've tried to do is give you a layman's understanding of the difference between legitimate MLM businesses and illegal pyramids and schemes. The information here should be quite sufficient to the average distributor.

For company executives, or those looking for a more detailed explanation, by all means you should seek out a law firm that specializes in the industry. I recommend Grimes & Reese, a firm that works extensively with Network Marketing. They were extremely helpful to me during the writing of this book. You can find them at http://www.mlmlaw.com.

Choosing your program...

Okay, now that you have a basic understanding of what constitutes a legitimate MLM company, how do you select the right one for you?

This is one of the most important decisions you will make in your network marketing career. Unfortunately, most people spend less time selecting a company than they do buying a new refrigerator. In fact, most let the company select them. There are two schools of thought on this.

First, if you're presented an opportunity by someone you know and trust—and they'd like to sponsor you and are committed to working with you—there's a good deal of power in that. It's not necessary for you to go out and discover every other network marketing company in the industry and do a side-by-side comparison. You would spend two years on research—and about the time you should be receiving some serious income, you'd be just getting started.

However, the company you join does play a dramatic role in your chances for success. You need to do enough due diligence to select a good one. Let me give you two questions to ask first. This will simplify things for you a great deal. If a company doesn't give you a positive answer to both of these questions, you can cross it off your list immediately.

1) If you were not involved in the business opportunity, would you buy this product or service anyway?

Be honest with yourself. If the answer is no, find another company. If the opportunity you're involved with is not centered on products you believe in and will personally use, it is highly unlikely that you will be successful with this company. Network Marketing is driven by the enthusiasm and personal testimonials of the people involved.

Two of the first things your prospects will ask you are whether the products are any good and you use them yourself. If you can't answer with an enthusiastic "yes" to both, they are not likely to get involved.

2) Would you buy that product or service *at that price?*

If you wouldn't pay the price for your products on the open market, it's unlikely anyone else will. Don't think people will pay more for a product simply because they might get a bonus check. It's been shown time and time again they won't.

Your success in MLM is based upon getting your products to the end consumers who actually use them and reorder them often. People who buy products just to get a bonus check end up stockpiling them and will eventually stop buying when their garage is full or their credit card is maxed out.

People must be willing to pay the retail price for your products. However, this doesn't mean your company must have products cheaper than what's available somewhere else. It means that the products must be of such value that you and other people are willing to pay the price for them.

In fact, many network marketing companies have products that cost more than similar products available elsewhere. But due to their high quality, effectiveness, or concentration, they actually offer better value to the consumer.

Network marketers have introduced a large number of products to the general public that would never have stood a chance in the traditional distribution system—products like pycnogenol, oral chelation, enzymes, antioxidant juices and gels, and other products that need the conversational marketing that Network Marketing does best. These products have helped millions of people and even saved and extended lives.

And companies like Amway, Shaklee, and Melaleuca were promoting concentrated products with green packaging decades before these ideas reached popular consciousness. Network Marketing also led the field with more all-natural products long before they were trendy.

Of course, the other tangible advantage is the personalized service and attention a customer receives from MLM distributors. Customers are willing to pay a little more for this personalized service and convenience. So don't worry about whether you have the cheapest product on the market, just whether the product is a good value.

Let's look at the other product variables you should be considering as you evaluate a company.

Are the products unique and exclusive?

Ideally, you want products that are available exclusively from your company, so your customers can get them only from you. If products just like yours are for sale in retail stores or online, you're likely to face more challenges unless your price point is dramatically lower.

Are they consumable?

I'm biased here, but I think consumable products like vitamins, skin care, personal care, and cleaning products work better long-term than non-consumables like water purifiers, air filters, or jewelry. I know our business is filled with nutritional and household products and personal care companies, but there's a reason for that: It works.

If your people use up shampoo, laundry soap, or vitamins on a continuous basis (as the kind of people you want to be around do), you're likely to experience more frequent orders. This means higher volumes and bigger residual bonus checks for you.

What kind of monthly volumes are likely to be produced by the products you market?

This is an important question because a great

31

deal of your volume is going to be produced by the personal consumption of your network participants. And, of course, the rest will come from the monthly consumption of their customers. *The higher the monthly average is, the bigger your profit potential will be.*

Suppose you're in a company with only one product, an energy drink that sells for $40 and the average person uses one bottle a month. With 100 distributors and customers in your organization, you would get paid on a volume of $4,000.

Now suppose you're in a company with an energy drink, meal replacement bars, a multi-vitamin, antioxidants, and fiber caplets. And the average monthly volume per family is $100. With the same 100 distributors and customers, you would be receiving override commissions on a volume of $10,000. All things being equal, you're going to make more money in a multiple products company. Of course, this means you make more retail profits as well.

This doesn't mean you can't make money in a one-product company. If the product has a high-dollar monthly cost, or if people need to buy it a lot during a month, you'll produce and get paid on higher volumes.

But the bottom line is the higher your average monthly product usage is, the greater your profit potential will be.

These product questions are the foremost considerations you should have as you choose a company. Real long-term organizational growth is driven by product demand. The compensation plan, company leadership, and other factors are all secondary to the product.

There are opportunists and even some trainers out there who will tell you that the products don't matter. They insist that the compensation plan is what drives growth. This may be true initially (when the hype machine is in full swing), but you cannot sustain your business long-term if your products are not a good value for the consumer. This is a lesson I learned personally...

About 15 years ago, I was just starting to make some money in the business. I attended a seminar put on by an author who had written a book on MLM. In a private conversation, he told me that the products were really irrelevant; it was the compensation plan that drove growth. He said we could all buy the products each month and throw them in the river. As long as everyone purchased the minimum each month, we'd all make money.

Being young and gullible, and figuring he was the expert, I took his advice to heart.

At that time, I was working with a program that allowed you to buy gift certificates in lieu of a monthly product purchase. Since the monthly volume I needed to qualify was $100, I bought a gift certificate for that amount each month.

This was when I still smoked, back when you could do so in public places without getting shot or arrested. So each month, at my biggest opportunity meeting, I would light a cigarette with a gift certificate and let the audience watch it burn up. What a showstopper!

I would explain that I had paid $100 for the gift certificate and tell them how much my check was that month (which was about $10,000). I went on to say that as long as I bought $100 worth of stuff—even if

I burned up a gift certificate or bought products and threw them away—I would get a check! I thought this logic was unassailable. It was.

Except for two slight problems.

Number one, it was illegal. As you now know, any deal where people buy simply to qualify for a check is considered a pyramid—illegal in most countries around the world.

And number two is the fact that it completely diminishes the value of products. People view products simply as a means to get a fast paycheck, so they never even use them. They don't bond to them; they miss the emotional connection so critical to long-term success.

It is this emotional connection to your company's products that motivates people to grow and also keeps them from jumping to the next hot deal that comes along.

But I didn't know all this back then. So I burned my gift certificates and preached the power of the profit incentive. And, of course, my frontline leaders duplicated me. Hell, even some of the nonsmokers took up the habit so they too could burn certificates at their opportunity meetings!

Everything worked great for about five or six levels down, because these people were all making, or about to make, more than their $100 monthly expense. The problems began on the lower levels, where people were not yet in profit...

The end of the month came and went, but these people never placed an order. When the bonus checks came out, their surprised and frustrated sponsor would call them up, demanding to know why they hadn't ordered anything.

"Because I don't have anyone under me yet" was the reply.

Well, of course, the next month those sponsors might not order, because the people under them might not be ordering, because they didn't have volume under them. Attrition started at the bottom and began to work its way up, level by level. This organization, which had taken me more than a year of hard work to build, looked like it was going to self-destruct in a couple of months.

It took a lot of frantic scrambling to stop the bleeding. I got back to personally using the products and conducted product workshops and other activities to show the value of the products. The products matter. They must be the driving catalyst for the company.

An interesting side note...

I came to learn that the "expert" on MLM, by whom I had been influenced, was actually just another opportunist with no regard for others. He used his books and seminars to raid people from other organizations. He was actually in 20 or 30 companies at a time. He would roll all his people into a new company, taking himself to the top of the pay plan within a few months.

Meanwhile, all the other distributors in this new company would be wondering how he had accomplished this growth so fast. So they'd buy his books and tapes and go to his seminars, hoping to learn his secret. They would follow the methods taught in the materials, only to find that they didn't work. They were theories. The trainer himself never actually used these methods to build a group. He built his groups only by raiding the organizations of others.

About the time the people in this new company discovered that his methods didn't work, our trainer was ready to move on to the next company. He would explain that the reason his methods weren't working was because the opportunity was flawed. But, fortunately—and here was the good news—he had just discovered a better one!

So off he would go to another new deal, taking some of the people from the old one with him. And bringing his larger group to this new deal would shoot him up to the top of the pay plan once again...and he would duplicate the entire process all over again.

Believe it or not, there are actually so many start-up companies always popping up and closing down that he's done this for over 20 years. He's made millions selling training materials and seminars to unsuspecting souls.

There are a couple of lessons here. First, find a company that makes sense and stick with it. Never turn your ethics and reasoning ability over to anyone else. If something doesn't make sense to you or seems unethical... pass it up. The only free cheese is in the mousetrap.

This doesn't mean you can't learn things from outside experts. It does mean you should discuss what you learn from them with your sponsorship line—because they have a vested interest in your success.

Okay, let's assume that all of the product issues are resolved. What are the other factors important in selecting the right company for you?

Begin with your sponsorship line. Select them as you would any other business partner.

They are going to be your coaches and your support structure, and you're going to be spending a lot of time with them in the next two to four years. After that you'll hopefully be spending the next 30 or 40 years taking cruises and vacations with them at resorts around the world.

There is a pervasive belief that if you are a moral person, you are compelled to sign up under whoever sold you that first bottle of product or first mentioned the name of the company to you. That makes as much sense as saying you are morally obligated to build your franchise on the first vacant property you see, even if it is out in the country. This is serious business in which you need to make intelligent, well-informed choices.

It's important that your sponsor be someone you like, trust, and would enjoy working with. Don't think you must sponsor in with someone who's making a big check or is a "heavy hitter." The qualities above are much more important. In fact, in cases of rapid growth...your best sponsor might be someone who's not yet making $300 a month!

This is because in an organization that is "moving on" (the kind you want to be in), it's not unusual for it to go down four or five levels in depth in a single month. These new people don't yet have experience or big checks, but they have the drive, vision, and enthusiasm necessary to build an organization.

However, you do want to make sure there is some experience at the top of the organization somewhere. You want someone who has already successfully accomplished what you are looking to do.

If you're going to fly to Hawaii from California, you're better off doing it with a pilot that has actually flown a real plane, not just played with computer simulations.

Look for a sponsorship line with a step-by-step system in place. The system should include the recruiting process, product training, "get started" training, live events, and conference calls or webcasts for ongoing training.

This information should be specifically spelled out and available to everyone in the organization. It should explain what action to take and what materials to use at each step of the recruiting and sponsoring process.

This is important to you for two reasons:

First, it will greatly speed up the time it takes you to build your group. By having a system that outlines exactly what to do, you won't spend time wondering what to do next or waste valuable time pursuing strategies that don't work. Such a system includes only those methods and techniques that have proven themselves and stood the test of time.

The second reason a system is so important to you is it ensures that the people you introduce into the business will be able to duplicate your success. Their education level or their business experience ceases to be an issue. They simply follow the system exactly as you (and your sponsorship line) did.

If the company you're looking at has a system, but your potential sponsorship line doesn't follow it, your group will forever be receiving mixed messages and growth will be difficult.

If the company doesn't have a real system (and most don't), but the sponsorship line does, you can achieve success fairly readily. The perfect situation is finding both a company and sponsorship line in sync with a duplicable system.

Finally, after all these other factors, you can start to look at the specifics of the company...

Conventional wisdom says you should look for a seasoned company, one that's at least five years old and debt-free. Let's look at that.

The truth is most new network marketing companies will go out of business within two years. Of course, it's also true that most new restaurants, dry cleaners, and valet parking companies will go out of business within two years as well. That's the nature of business in the entrepreneurial system—90 percent of start-ups fail. Network Marketing is no better and no worse. So, does that mean you should avoid start-ups? Maybe.

The odds that a start-up company will go out of business are greater than those of a ten-year-old, well-established company. Yet, there is a certain allure to start-up companies—a chance to "get in on the ground floor"—that attracts people. If the company has a founders club, or similar program, you could get in early and qualify for very lucrative bonus pools that will not be available in later years.

A company that's new and not yet known has a tremendous growth potential. You have the possibility of greater risk—and the corresponding opportunity for greater rewards.

On the other hand, working with a household name gives you a certain amount of credibility to begin with and you're likely to face less skepticism.

I have worked with established companies and enjoyed moderate success. I joined two start-up companies on the ground floor only to find out later there was a basement! But I also joined a company in pre-launch that has gone on to become a serious player and made me millions of dollars, and in which I was able to create a legacy position for myself. Which option is right for you depends a lot on your personality.

If you're not adverse to a certain degree of risk, you may enjoy the challenges of a start-up opportunity and the chance to cash in big time as you ride a new company to the top. If you're more conservative and looking for greater security, go with an established company. You'll face less risk and probably experience more stable growth. Choose the situation that best matches your personality.

Now let's deal with this issue of being debt-free...

Truth is, about the only companies that advertise they are debt-free are start-ups with credit so bad they can't qualify for credit anyway. Or they are growing so slowly they don't need to be in debt. And then there are those who do have debt and are lying about it.

Just about every company that experiences rapid expansion will experience cash flow problems and need a line of credit to continue to grow. This is true not just in Network Marketing, but in any business. In fact, due to the exponential growth often experienced in this business, you could argue the case that there's even more reason to have a line of credit in Network Marketing than traditional companies.

In the early 1990s, I was building a program that put in over 25,000 new, active distributors and customers in one month. Two months later, we put in 40,000 new, active people in a month. A short time later, 60,000 in one month.

The kinds of demands made on the parent company during exponential growth like this are mind-boggling. To expand phone lines fast enough, to find and hire enough employees, and to simply locate and lease office space to keep up with the demand are monumental challenges.

Now, figure what it takes to keep up with production in manufacturing products. Factories can't be built in two months. It can take a year to find the right site, draw up the plans, and pull the permits. Realistically, you have to start planning a factory three to five years before you need it. Depending upon the breadth of the product line, machinery at the factory can cost tens of millions of dollars.

So imagine having to add 100 or more employees a month; pay for all the phones, office space, desks, computers, training, etc., that they require; and invest tens of millions of dollars more in a factory that you won't need for two or three years. This is the challenge a fast-growing network marketing company faces. The company that can finance this kind of growth out of cash flow is one in a million. And you could actually argue that to do so would leave the company's assets too tied up to handle any unexpected challenges that arise.

I hate debt. I was burdened with it for too many years. Nowadays, I try to encourage my people to pay cash for everything, including their cars, and even pay off their mortgage. Yet it still makes sense to keep a line of credit or some credit cards. While you may not use that credit, having it available makes sense. The same holds true for companies.

Imagine the dilemma placed on a network marketing company in the heat of exponential growth. Being completely debt-free might not be a good idea at all. I have seen this happen time and time again—companies grow so fast, they grow themselves out of business. Even as fast as they're growing, the money coming in is simply not sufficient to adequately finance the massive ramp-up in physical plant and operations that's necessary.

This does not mean the company shouldn't be properly capitalized. I believe the days when a successful network marketing company could be started in a basement or on a kitchen table are over. It takes at least $15 million in start-up capital to launch a company today, because the Internet makes the whole world a neighborhood marketplace.

Even with this kind of start-up cash, it's likely that when the company hits "critical mass" and enters the exponential growth curve, it will need a line of credit or an infusion of more money to keep ahead of demand on production, personnel, manufacturing facilities, and offices.

A company with some debt and creditworthiness with a financial institution is a good sign. So all told, finding a company that's debt-free is simply a non-issue. As far as the other things to look for from the company standpoint, here's what I think are important:

Management Depth

If the entire corporate staff consists of five people, the company will be hard pressed to give any meaningful type of distributor support. A credible company should have a president and CEO (which may be the same person), a chief financial officer, a chief operations officer, an administrative manager, a distribution center manager, a data processing chief, a customer service manager, and a marketing vice president or manager.

Some of these positions, even in a brand new, start-up company, will require assistants and line employees. There may not be much for them to do when the company first opens. But the whole point in business is having the resources you need before you need them.

I especially look at what kind of marketing staff a company has. Do they have a marketing VP or national marketing manager? Do they have corporate trainers who travel around to the functions and conduct training? Is there a support staff to back up these people? What kind of customer service department do they have?

It's important to know if anyone on the corporate management staff has any successful network marketing experience. Networking is dramatically different from traditional business, even direct sales. If a management team doesn't understand the unique nature of Network Marketing, it will be quite difficult for them to guide the company.

When I consult with companies, this is the biggest issue they face. They have a management team with corporate experience who try to force selling techniques in a network marketing culture.

Compensation Plan...

In the earlier editions of this book, I broke down the different types of compensation plans and looked at the benefits and drawbacks of each. I have removed that information from this edition for two reasons.

First, the information is too complex for the average distributor or prospect to understand. And second, today there are so many plans that are hybrids of the four basic plans, this no longer makes sense. Instead you are better off focusing on the results being produced by the plan you're looking at.

You want a compensation plan to do certain things.

These include:

- Allow a new distributor to earn some start-up money quickly;
- Provide some transitional income to bridge people during the time they are gaining experience and developing their skill sets;
- Provide a platform to create passive income;
- Offer "sexy" perks like contests, trips, and bonus cars;
- Compensate top producers with incomes that keep them in the fold; and most importantly,
- Reward people for practicing the proper behavior.

Here are the reasons for the above...

People today are broke! Savings are at an all-time low, while debt is at an all-time high. And people are impatient! The days when they would stick around while making $15 a month are over. Most will have to put the start-up investment on their credit card, and they will need to earn it back quickly.

For the same reason, they need transitional income. This doesn't have to be huge. As long as they are earning something, say $300 or $500 a month, that will allow them to invest in the business by purchasing marketing materials, attending events, and getting their products paid for. This will keep them in the fold until they learn what they need to know to reach the high incomes and other perks.

The third reason is based on a personal bias of mine. I always look for what elements of the plan can provide true passive income. I don't want to have to do things over and over each month. That's why I don't work at Pizza Hut any longer. I want to do the job once, do it right, and continue to get paid every month. And there are a lot of other people like me.

The reason for the perks is they make recruiting so much easier for the average distributor. But distributors don't always realize this...

If you ask most people if they would rather get $3,000 or a free trip to Hawaii, they'll opt for the cash. Then they'll pay bills with the money, and it will be gone in 48 hours. But give them a trip to an exotic locale, and they will be snapping pix, taking videos, and reliving that trip for years. It creates a lifetime experience that is anchored with your company.

When I consult with companies on designing comp plans, I always include these types of goodies, because they have a very real effect of recruiting, improving retention, and contributing to distributor satisfaction.

When someone wins a cruise or other free trip, everyone they know hears about it. When you drive home in a new car and your neighbors find out you got it for free, they're breathless to know how. So building these perks into the plan is one of the best investments a company can make.

Now that leaves us with two major issues the comp plan must address: how it is balanced, both in relation to paying people at the various levels and rewarding them for taking the proper behavior. These two issues are interrelated.

First, we want the plan to give people incentives for doing the right thing. So it should not be skewed so all the money comes from bonuses provided by the volume produced by the initial enrollment orders. You want people working to produce volume all of the time. And it's very important that the plan pays leaders for working down the organization in depth. This ensures that new distributors will get the support they need from experienced leaders.

The real nuance is providing the proper balance between the top and bottom of the pay plan. Some plans are "top heavy."

An example might be plans for companies that have only one or two products but have a high dollar level (like ten or fifteen thousand dollars a month) that distributors must maintain to receive overrides on their directors that break away. Due to the lower average volumes they actually achieve, 99 percent of the distributors will never consistently qualify.

In binary plans this may be evidenced by most of the commissions earned in the "running legs," so new people earn almost nothing.

In top-heavy plans most of the overrides roll up to a few poster boys and poster girls or are considered "breakage," and the money washes up to the company.

This can produce high six-figure monthly incomes for these poster kids at the top of the plan. But for each of these big earners, there are tens of thousands of distributors not making a monthly check big enough to take their family to the movies. These big distributors can wave their mega checks around to hype growth initially, but ultimately most distributors will move on once they discover that they are not likely to earn any serious money. They will leave with a bad taste in their mouth and believe that MLM doesn't work.

On the other hand, bottom-heavy plans will not work well long-term either. These are plans where virtually anyone who joins can get high profits with minimal effort. They are designed in a way that over-rewards new people, with the hope that this will attract distributors from other companies to jump ship and come to the new company.

This excites people initially, but in the long term, the top leaders cannot make the incomes they deserve. You only have a finite amount of money to pay out. If you're overpaying the people on the bottom, it's coming out of the pockets of the people at the top. These people look at other plans and realize that with the exact same volume and same organization, they would make a lot more money in another company. This creates a leadership drain that ultimately prevents a company from succeeding.

To really balance a plan is a science. You want the beginning distributor to be able to start earning profit as quickly as possible, yet have the plan allow leaders to build up to and maintain big-dollar incomes. Depth should be paid in proportion to width.

If this plan is properly constructed, it contains all of the necessary elements to promote growth and pay people in proportion to the work they've actually done.

One more thought before I leave the subject...

I'm afraid we have become jaded. If someone isn't pulling in at least $30,000 or $40,000 a month, we almost look on that as a failure.

Yet we know that 80 or 90 percent of the bankruptcies today could be averted with a mere $300 or $400 a month in income.

Personally I have tens of thousands of distributors in places like Russia, Ukraine, Singapore, Nigeria, and other places where $500 or $1,000 a month makes a HUGE difference in their standard of living. And given the current economic meltdown going on at the time I'm writing this, you can argue that these modest bonus checks would also still make a huge difference to millions of people even in the U.S., the U.K., and other developed nations.

In today's difficult economy, Network Marketing is providing a lifeline of financial security to millions. Most companies are paying out somewhere between 35 to 50 percent of their sales into their compensation plans. That means commissions of at least $40 BILLION are being paid out annually to distributors around the world.

Most people are not going to be earning $50,000 a month in the business. They're not willing to do the self-development and work that entails. But as long as the plan rewards them relative to what they do, then it's fair.

Remember even those $300 and $400 bonus checks are buying groceries, funding schools, paying for medicine, supporting charities, making car payments, and keeping mortgages current. Let's not lose sight of that.

Now, let's look at some other considerations you should take into account when choosing a company.

Support Structure:

What kind of support structure is in place? Does the company you're considering put out a monthly newsletter? Does the newsletter list achievements, feature products, and have business-building information? Or is it simply a collection of miracle-cure product testimonials that are likely to get the company closed down by regulators?

Are there annual conventions, leadership training programs, and other events hosted by the company? Do they have regularly scheduled conference calls or webcasts? Are the materials professionally prepared, benefit-driven, and effective from a marketing standpoint? Do they maintain a comprehensive website, and are there provisions for you to have your own offshoot from the site?

This is where I see most companies fall down. And I do mean most companies, not just the start-up ones. There are two major problems, which I see repeated time and time again.

Problem Number One...

All of the company materials are completely devoted to the products—and the business opportunity is either not mentioned or mentioned as an afterthought. You see this a lot, because most network marketing company managers don't understand the true nature of the business. They don't comprehend the concept of duplication (though I have yet to meet one who will admit this), and they think it's a sales business.

As a result, they keep producing pretty product brochures, videos, and audios, and exhorting their distributor force with silly platitudes like "These products just sell themselves." There's nothing to tell the prospect how the business works, how money is made, or even what the business is. The next time someone tells you their products just sell themselves, you might reply, "Well, in that case, you won't be needing me!"

Problem Number Two...

All of the marketing materials are feature-driven, not benefit-driven. Here's the distinction:

Anything about your company, products, or comp plan is a *feature*. Anything about the prospect is a *benefit*. Prospects are motivated to action by benefits. Yet, interestingly enough, in 90 percent of the marketing materials I see, you couldn't find a benefit in them with a search party.

Look at the materials of the company you're considering. Is the first thing you see the company logo? A picture of the founder? Pictures of the air handlers on the top of the manufacturing facility? Are they filled with inane blather about how great they are, how old they are, where their officers went to school, and where they travel to get ingredients for the products? These things are all features and mean nothing to your prospects.

I know a company that spent $250,000 producing a recruiting video completely devoted to showing the machines that make capsules, the machines that put the capsules into bottles, the machines that cap the bottles, and the machines that load the bottles into boxes. What prospect could possibly care less about such silliness?

Make it about the prospect...

Marketing materials, in order to be effective, must be about the prospect. This means the materials are benefit-driven, not feature-driven.

If your brochure says, "We're an established, eleven-year-old company," that's a feature. If it says, "Your future is secure, because we're an established, eleven-year-old company," now we're getting to benefits.

If your materials claim, "We have an automobile fund," that's a feature. If they say, "When you reach the Gold Director rank, you'll get a new car for free," that's a benefit.

Here's a helpful way to know if something is a feature versus a benefit. If you can put the words "you get" at the front of the sentence, it's probably a benefit. If you can't, more than likely it's not.

The effectiveness of the marketing materials you have to work with will dramatically impact your success, so evaluate them carefully.

The final factor to consider when choosing a company is how well they do the basics. If a company does not ship product in a timely manner nor pay commissions on time every month, my advice is to move on. My experience is that if a company does not have the capital and resources to pay bills and stock product early on, these problems will only get worse as the company gets bigger.

Even the best companies experience problems with

inventory from time to time as they try to keep up with demand. While no one enjoys problems, these are the kind you like to have. If a company is generally well run and ships out *the vast majority of its orders* on time, an occasional miscue should be overlooked. But when a company consistently does not ship in a timely manner nor pay its bills or commission checks when due, that is a sure sign of trouble.

Final thoughts on selecting a company...

You'll notice in every case, I used the singular not the plural when talking about choosing a company. I don't believe anyone can build two or more programs simultaneously. This is a big issue with "MLM junkies." They're in so many crazy deals all the time, one or more of them is always in the process of going bust. They use this as evidence that they should be in yet more deals—to diversify and protect their income. And they offer all sorts of convoluted logic to support this position.

"Company A has nutrition products—Company B has household cleaners, so they don't compete with each other. You need to use the phone for both of them, so Company C—a long distance program—is the perfect complementary program. And Company D offers a free car program—which is perfect—because Company E sells car wax!"

Ah, no. Even with two companies whose products do not compete, the business opportunity does.

A Shell service station franchisee wouldn't open an Exxon station across the street. It would be foolish. Why compete with yourself?

Now, you can find a few people who get income

from more than one program. But my experience has been that if the income is substantial, it was produced by the person working one program at a time. In other words, he or she built up one program and retired. Later, he or she joined another company and built a new network, never touching their people in the first organization. If you want to build a vacation home, it doesn't make sense to use the boards from your existing house.

Working more than one program can look tempting. Discounts on all those products. All those bonus checks coming in. All those different cars, trips, and awards you're going to win...

In actuality, those things don't happen. Each company's system contradicts the other. There are so many materials to buy, functions to attend, and training systems to learn that your distributors become confused. They're paralyzed into inactivity.

Take the time necessary to select the right program for you—then give it everything you've got, exclusively.

Chapter Four:

How a System Helps You Succeed

In the 1970s, franchising revolutionized the business world. The concept—quite controversial at the time—was that the parent company (franchiser) would provide a complete business system, including site selection, operating procedures, purchasing requirements, and employee training. They offered this expertise and complete business model for an upfront investment and ongoing royalties on sales.

The person who licensed the business (franchisee) gave up a percentage of the profits but dramatically increased his or her chance of business success. These franchises were dubbed "turn key" businesses, because you were supposed to be able to just turn the key, unlock the front door, and be open and ready for business. There were step-by-step procedures to follow for each facet of the business, from the simplest detail (what brand of straws to use) to the most complex (how to lay out the kitchen equipment for maximum productivity).

McDonald's, of course, is the consummate example of a successful franchise. Go to any of their stores at 7 o'clock in the evening and you're likely to find it being run by a 19- or 20-year-old who just recently graduated from teenage acne. It's possible this kid has a mother who won't let him borrow her Volvo because she doesn't trust him with it. Yet, this same kid is successfully running an operation that does in excess of $3 million a year in sales. What's the secret?

The secret is the system...

One of the most complete, specific, and tested systems ever developed. A system that can turn any 15-year-old into an effective, efficient, and productive employee. One to three items go in this bag; four to six items go in the next size bag; these are the napkins to use; here's where to buy them; place the order each week on this day; and this is when they'll be delivered.

You see the same thing in the military. Nineteen-year-old kids are flying fighter jets that cost more than the gross national product of developing countries. But there's a pre-flight checklist, an in-flight checklist, a post-flight checklist, and probably a checklist just for the checklists.

Having this kind of system to follow created a quantum leap in the success ratios of start-up businesses. Today, as then, franchises have a dramatically higher level of success than independent businesses.

In the 1970s, a similar metamorphosis took place in Network Marketing. The business, which had been almost the exclusive domain of blue-collar workers, started to attract some more white-collar professionals. The old-school distributors mostly looked at the business as a sales business, with many actually going door-to-door. But the new people realized the power of leverage, worked relentlessly towards duplication, and saw this new occupation not as a part-time job, but as something that could replace their income or even their job or career and become a true profession. The thing that made the difference was the concept of a duplicable system.

A system is the road map to how success is created in

your company. It should completely delineate the entire process that a distributor will follow: where to find prospects, how to approach them, how to sponsor them, and how to train them to reach the higher pin ranks. (For the sake of simplicity and your understanding, I'll use the term "pin ranks" throughout this book. This means people who reach the top levels of your compensation plan, whether they're called Diamond Directors, National Vice Presidents, or Master Coordinators. The name comes from the fact that distributors usually receive a pin upon achieving these ranks.) Each stage in this process should be clearly defined and taught to the distributor at the appropriate time.

Before getting into specifics, I want to discuss the formula for creating true duplication and wealth in our business. It may strike you as simplistic, but I promise you it is actually quite profound. This formula is where duplication lives. It is:

"Lead a large group of people—to consistently do a few simple actions—over a sustained period of time."

You'll notice there are three sections that make up the formula. First is the large group of people. You need enough critical mass to get traction and for duplication to take off.

The second element is to have those people perform only a few actions and to keep those actions simple. One of the biggest mistakes newcomers make is to try and quantify everything, and in doing so they add too much complexity. For true duplication we need to focus on actions simple enough that everyone in the large group can replicate.

And finally, you need this to happen over a sustained period of time. I believe building a solid network is a two- to four-year plan. Mark Yarnell says five, and he's one of the brightest minds in the business.

So it doesn't happen in a month or two or even six. We need people to consistently take the actions for a sustained period of time. This is how wealth is created in MLM.

The next thing that's important for you to understand is how you get that formula happening in your team. It doesn't come from speaking or training it. *It comes from modeling the behavior.* What your people see you actually **do** is what they will duplicate.

The other thing vital for your system is the principle of higher source.

This principle is built around the fact that everything a distributor tells a potential prospect or another team member should come from a source higher than him- or herself. (Although I'm not referring to the Almighty, any upline support you receive from Divine sources is fine by me.). I mean a third-party tool. Something such as a DVD, CD, magazine, website, conference call, webcast, or even a story.

By always referring to a third-party tool (higher source), you ensure a better degree of duplication, because any new distributor can repeat the process much easier.

A product question that is answered with a brochure, an inquiry about the comp plan that is explained on the website, or a question about the company that is answered by a three-way call can be replicated by anyone at almost any level of experience. We often joke in our organization that "If you're with a prospect and your lips are moving, you better be pointing to a third-party tool."

I believe there are six necessary components for duplicating the system. They are:

1) Mass Market Recruiting Tool
2) Warm Market Introduction Tool
3) Standardized Presentation
4) Specified "Ladder of Escalation"
5) Standardized "Fast Start" Training
6) Training Event Structure

Let's look at each of these a little deeper.

The mass market recruiting tool is the resource that distributors use with the masses. Say they meet a sharp flight attendant, an efficient waiter, or anyone else they might come across in the course of their daily life who impresses them in some way. This tool is the first step in approaching these prospects.

I prefer a tool—as opposed to an invitation to an event—because I believe this helps up the duplication results. It's easier to get someone you don't know well to review a tool than it is to get that person to agree to attend a meeting. And the opening conversation is easier to learn. This tool could be a magazine, brochure, CD, DVD, or combination of the above.

The second component is a tool that facilitates the sponsoring process for use with the warm market— meaning the people you have relationships with.

So this would be used with friends, neighbors, and relatives. Again the result you are seeking is the best possible duplication.

In some companies this tool may be the same as the mass market tool. In my company it is a different one, because we use home meetings as the first step in the process for warm market candidates. So we created a DVD that is a "plug and play" presentation for this purpose.

The logic behind this is as follows: While a casual acquaintance is more likely to review a tool than attend a meeting, someone you know well is just the opposite. They don't want to review the tool, because they'd rather have you just explain what it is all about. They often want to bombard you with questions on the spot. But that will slow down duplication. So, in my opinion, it's better to ask them to attend a meeting, with the idea that the meeting will be able to explain things you can't.

The third component to create the best duplication is a standardized presentation. This is the presentation that is done at the major opportunity meetings. You want it to be the same in all markets and on all levels.

Naturally each presenter provides his or her unique flair, personal stories, and humor. But the presentation should follow the same basic outline in all markets. This means leaders can travel thousands of miles or kilometers, work with a team dozens or even hundreds of levels below them, and still be offering the basic presentation outline followed by local leaders.

Likewise with our fourth component, a specified series of interactions we take a prospect through or a "Ladder of Escalation." I created this name because at each step of the process you want to escalate the exposure to the prospect, making it a bigger deal than it was in the previous step.

For example, the first exposure to someone could be the mass-market tool—perhaps a CD. The next step may be an invitation to a home meeting. There may only be five people there, but it would seem to be a bigger deal than just reviewing a CD alone.

The next step could bump up the person to a hotel meeting that hundreds of people attend, making it seem like a bigger opportunity than the home meeting was. After that, the person might escalate to a conference call or webcast with thousands of people connected. The dynamic created here is what the psychologists call "social proof," and each step leads the candidate closer to a decision.

Each time this person sees a presentation, it's bigger, better, and more impressive than the time before, and each time there are more people involved, making it seem to be a "safer" decision to make.

Companies that reach powerful exponential growth have this down to a science. Each step is delineated, each step is bigger than the preceding one, and each step has corresponding collateral marketing material to give to the prospect. This produces powerful results and duplication.

Our fifth component is a standardized "fast start" training that all new team members go through right after joining. There may be nothing more important for retention than this step. I have found that you make or break your new team members in the first two weeks, and the first 48 hours are critical. If you get them into action and they begin getting some results, they are likely to stay around. If they procrastinate and don't get into immediate action, odds are very strong they will drop out.

So this fast start training should include details on how to place orders, make enrollments, and perform basic business set-up procedures, such as opening a bank account, ordering business cards, having a dedicated phone line, etc. It should also take the new distributor through the process of making a candidate list, explain the sponsoring sequence, and then motivate that person to start contacting his or her first candidates quickly.

The ideal would be for your company to have customized training like this already in place. However if none is provided, I have developed a generic tool that will help you here. It is called the "Fast Track Pack," and it includes my *First Steps* booklet and the follow-along audios: *What You Need to Know First, Getting Started*, and *Secrets of a Dynamic Day*. It also comes with *Check Out the Biz*, a generic DVD presentation of an opportunity meeting. You can use these and supplement them with any other materials available from your company. (You can find the Pack available in the resource store located at NetworkMarketingTimes.com.)

The final component necessary for strong duplication is your training event structure. This is usually a combination of field-sponsored and company-provided events, such as the annual convention. I believe that the field needs a major event each quarter to keep them inspired, focused, and properly trained. We'll look at this a little deeper in later chapters.

These six components are the foundation for creating solid, ongoing duplication in your team. As you set up these components, you want to keep three principles in mind. You are looking for ways you can *systemize them, automate them, and make them scalable.* Once you do that, you are well on your way to a true passive income and no longer essential to the process. Even if you back away from the business at a later date, the system keeps perpetuating itself.

Most people, even some successful ones in Network Marketing, don't have a system. It's because they built a network based upon their sales talents, or they give great meetings, or they use the sheer strength of personality. They mail 20 cards a day; they call all their key people five times a day; they hold rah-rah rallies all the time; or they are 24-hour-a-day sponsoring machines.

I know of a person who prospects 30 people a day. These kinds of people sponsor dozens and dozens of distributors a year—which they need to replace the dozens and dozens who drop out. They walk across the stage at their company conventions; they make lots of money; they live in nice houses; and they drive nice cars. But they certainly aren't living the lifestyle of freedom and controlling their own destiny. They've traded enslavement to a boss for enslavement to a business.

What these people do works. It just doesn't duplicate. They work hard and mean well, but the average person cannot duplicate what they are doing to build their businesses. Now granted, they're probably making a lot more money in their networking enslavement than they were making in their job—but they're still enslaved. More importantly, they can't show other people how to escape the rat race, because they're still trapped in it.

With a complete duplicable system, anyone—sales type or non-sales type, shy or outgoing—can do the business. The most important axiom in the business to remember is this:

It's not "Does it *work?*" but "Does it *duplicate?*"

Let me give you an example. Let's suppose you took an ad on the Super Bowl or World Cup broadcast to sign up new distributors. You could perhaps sign up 10,000 distributors in one night. But how many of them would have the two million dollars it takes to run a commercial on a program like those? Maybe one or two of them. And you know what they would do between now and the next Super Bowl? Nothing.

So the scenario above *works*. It signs up 10,000 people. But it doesn't *duplicate*.

How you bring in your people is how they will bring in their people.

Now this leads us to an issue I might as well address now and get it out of the way: the distinction between the two business models in Network Marketing.

When I wrote *The MLM Revolution*, my manifesto on the profession, I exposed the biggest lie in this business to be selling big business results by promoting small business tactics. This is a pandemic in the business and it stems from our failure to educate people on the difference between the small business retailer model and the big business duplication model. And most of the guilty parties aren't even aware they're misleading prospects, because they don't know the difference.

How many idiots do we have going around putting *"Millionaire looking for apprentices"* flyers on windshields in shopping center parking lots? How many clueless neophytes are running around placing yard signs at intersections, thinking this is going to build them a $50K-a-month bonus check?

Now there are certainly millionaires looking for apprentices (I'm one and probably many of you reading this are too), and a good number of us make $50K a month or even multiples of that. But we didn't get there by wearing cheesy buttons, handing out flyers at the mall, or driving around with magnetic signs on our Lamborghinis.

That doesn't mean that there is anything wrong with people who build with buttons, bumper stickers, or flyers. I'm just saying it won't build you a large team, which is the result we're looking for with this book.

If your main interest is to get your own products paid for or earn a few hundred or few thousand dollars a month, these tactics will work. But they won't create strong duplication or produce large bonus checks.

So you don't want to recruit on the basis of free cars, award trips, and large incomes—and then teach people that these peddler tactics are going to produce them. They're not. Not now. Not ever. The five- and six-figure monthly incomes are created by building the big business duplication model I'm teaching you here, not the "share the products with your friends" model many people are suggesting.

Back to the duplicable system...

When you first meet with people, the way to produce the strongest results is to lead with the business opportunity. If they are not interested in the business aspect, then you fall back on the outcome of getting them as a customer. That will produce better duplication than if you lead with your product or service first, then try to back into the business. Here's why:

Suppose you're in Mona Vie, Xango, or Usana and you sponsor a chiropractor. He thinks, *"These are great wellness products. They will help all my patients. I'll sell them in my practice."*

That works. But it doesn't duplicate well. What you find in this scenario is that the doctor will retail a lot of product. But it's unlikely he will duplicate down very many levels.

Even though he may talk to people about the business, 90 percent of them will never get involved. Even if the business sounds enticing, on a subconscious level they'll be thinking to do it successfully they'll first need to become a chiropractor and have 30-40 patients a day to prescribe products to.

Lets the dental care products in her practice, the personal trainer who joins Agel to market the products in his gym, or the makeup artist that sells Arbonne or Nu Skin in the salon.

These tactics work, but they don't duplicate very well. If these people would practice a system of duplication that leads with the business opportunity, they will ultimately build a much larger organization, because the people they enroll have a better shot of replicating their results. A system is not just for your own benefit—it helps all your people as well.

Chapter Five:

The Core Qualities of a Network Marketing Professional

There are ten core qualities that the network marketers who are professionals follow. To be a true professional requires more than just "going core" yourself. It means you also create the culture where these core qualities become standard practice in your organization. As you schedule your time and decide with whom you will work, you want to give priority to the members on your team who are also committed to the core qualities. Let's look at them:

1) Be a product of the products

To go "core" means that if your company has a product, you would never buy a competing product for any reason—ever. A "Brand X" product purchase takes money out of your business and puts it into someone else's. If your company has an autoship program, you should be on it.

As a core person, you carry enough inventory so you never run out of product or have to buy a competing one. You are influenced by neither sales nor incentives, and you always buy from your own store. You must use all of your company's products that apply to you—and be able to talk knowledgeably and enthusiastically about those products to effectively build your business.

2) Develop a consumer group

Your business is driven by the volume produced by sales to the end consumer. As you know, a great deal of those sales will be to distributors who buy from their own store and use the products themselves. But there are many other people who will benefit from your products or services who are not interested in building a business at this time. These people will become your consumer group.

It's critical that you nurture and develop this group. This is good business, because you earn retail profits, develop residual income, and build your group volume that will qualify you for faster rank advancement and higher rewards. When you are just starting out, a good goal is to develop a base of at least ten retail customers.

3) Follow the system

I've already discussed this, so I won't belabor it here. Leaders understand that "lone rangers" can be successful initially, but will not enjoy long-term success. For residual income and walk-away security, you must follow a step-by-step duplicable system, and you yourself must be duplicable.

Your sponsorship line has learned what works and what doesn't. They have created the system based on that experience. When you follow the system, you have the resources of the entire sponsorship line working for you. If you change the system, you lose the benefits of having all those people and resources at your disposal. Also, when you change the system, you send a message to your people that it's okay to change the system, and after a few levels it no longer exists. Keep the system sacred.

4) Attend all events

Let's start with opportunity meetings. There are a lot of people out there claiming that opportunity meetings are no longer necessary, and they can be replaced by working phone leads, sending out emails, or placing advertising. I'm not buying it.

The truth is every company that has hit the exponential growth curve and then sustained substantial volume has done so with opportunity meetings. Even with picture phones, webcasts, and technology developing at an amazing rate, I doubt this will change any time soon, if ever. There is a certain magic that happens when you put a large group of people together in a ballroom.

Yes, conducting meetings takes more work than sitting at home in your bunny slippers working on the Internet. But the energy and social proof that a live meeting offers can't be found anywhere else.

How often the meetings are held vary from organization to organization. But when they are held in your area, you need to be there. And if there are no opportunity meetings in your market, your number one priority should be to help get them started.

You also need to be at the "major functions."

Functions are the glue that holds your business together. Attending them helps you grow your business, gives you crucial training, and keeps you focused. In your regional area, you will have the chance to attend product workshops, events, and rallies. If these are within four to five hours driving distance, you need to be there. There will be other events, such as conventions and leadership conferences, which are held annually. These are major, often life-changing events, and you'll want to schedule your vacation time around them so you'll never miss one.

Expect to get the most blow back from your new team members on this issue. They don't understand how important these events are and often are hesitant to buy plane tickets and attend events held long distances away. But your job as a leader is to practice some tough love and get them there. The skill sets they acquire and the belief and confidence they develop from these events produce dramatically higher incomes and make the investment more than worth it.

5. Be a student of the profession

If you want to build your business in the fastest manner possible, you must be teachable and willing to be coached. You will find Network Marketing is quite different from traditional businesses. Things that work great in sales or other businesses sometimes do not work well in Network Marketing.

Your sponsorship line has learned the methods, strategies, and techniques that work best in your business. They will work with you and teach you everything they know...for free. Your sponsor is the repository of all the experience of many generations of distributors—all the way to the company. Learn from him or her.

Make a conscious effort to learn all you can about

the profession as a whole. Subscribe to the professional publications, and study generic books and other resources about Network Marketing. You'll find some of these mentioned in the "Recommended Resources" section in the back of this book.

6) Be accountable

I've discussed the chain letters and money games that masquerade as legitimate network marketing programs. Because of them, we have to set a standard of integrity much higher than that of the corporate world. If something seems a little questionable, don't do it.

Network Marketing is a business of relationships, and relationships operate on trust. To earn and maintain that trust, you must be accountable.

You can never lie to your distributors or customers and remain accountable. Accountability also means that when you write checks, they're good; when you promise to work with someone, you follow through; and when you commit to attend an event, you're there, on time.

Accountability means that when we have a product display with 24 products, there will still be 24 products at the end of the night. It means never approaching someone else's prospect or attempting to steal distributors from another line.

7) Practice edification

Savvy distributors learn that they must edify their sponsorship line. By "edify" I simply mean to "build up." When you point out the success and accomplishments of your sponsors, it makes those sponsors more effective when they come to work with both your prospects and distributors.

Many times you will find it difficult to be a prophet in your own hometown. Sometimes your friends and relatives aren't yet ready to accept that powerful, positive concepts can come from you. By edifying your sponsorship line—then bringing your prospects into your home base—you'll have support to hold you over until you develop some initial success and credibility. (This is practicing the principle of higher source I discussed earlier.)

This was a lesson I had to learn the hard way. I was so ego-driven in my early years in the business that I would never edify my sponsor. In fact, I did quite the opposite.

I used to complain to all my people how weak my sponsor was, hoping I would look strong by comparison. (Of course, it did just the opposite, but I couldn't see that.) In any event, when my sponsor would come to town to do a training or conduct an opportunity meeting, few of my people would turn out. So when I needed someone to give me credibility, there was no one to provide that. I never got any of my close friends or family members in the business. I still believe today the reason is because I didn't edify my sponsorship line.

You should also edify the organization, your company, and the entire profession. Back in the day, I would spend a lot of time pointing out the shortcomings of competing companies, looking for a competitive advantage. These days I'd much rather edify them and the profession as a whole. I think this ultimately is more effective.

8) Commit to a weekly exposure number and do it

You can't control enrollments, but you can control how many people you offer the chance to look at the business. Make a commitment, such as exposing the business to two people a day, five days a week.

This doesn't mean you have to make that many presentations; you probably won't have enough time for that anyway. But you commit to offering a certain number of people a chance to look at your business. Some of these exposures could be introductory emails, a phone call, or handing a person a CD, magazine, or DVD. You simply expose others to the opportunity to gauge if there is serious interest there.

9) Spend daily self-development time

If I've discovered one fundamental truth, it is this: Your business will grow only as fast as you do. You will have to develop new skills as your business progresses. Initially the skills sets you need are about developing a candidate list, meeting people, and inviting. Later you'll need to develop presentation and follow-up skills. Ultimately, you will need to learn leadership development.

The early skills are more about business techniques, and the higher skills are more about interpersonal interaction.

It's important that you set aside specific time each day for self-development. For most people, this is best done in the morning before the day starts. You might meditate, exercise, listen to inspirational audios, or read books that help you grow your mind, body, and soul. Set aside this time and stick to it.

Invest in audios, books, and videos that help your personal development...and make sure half of this is specific to your network marketing business. Keep positive CDs in your car and listen to those instead of the noise and negative programming of the radio. Get an iPod and download inspirational material for when you go walking, jogging, or cycling.

Never end your day by watching the late news and then going to sleep. Make sure the last input you receive before going to bed is positive—even if it's just reading one paragraph from an inspirational book. (I keep "As a Man Thinketh" next to my bed, so I can read a paragraph from it first thing each morning and last thing each evening.)

Many companies or sponsorship lines offer programs that provide positive, inspirational, and/or instructional material on a subscription basis. If you're in such a situation, you are quite fortunate, because much of the work of finding and getting good material is already done for you. Sign up right away and make sure your people do as well.

10) Do the right thing at all times

Situations will arise where you may be conflicted as to what to do. Perhaps someone from another line approached you and wants to jump to your line. Maybe someone else's prospect gravitates toward you. At the end of the day, it's not that hard to know what is the right thing to do. Do it. Tell the truth, edify others, honor other team members' prospects, and do what you promise. Period.

These ten core qualities are what separate network marketing professionals from the amateurs. Practicing all the core qualities isn't always easy—it's not supposed to be. But if you're truly interested in building a successful network that others can duplicate, they're vital.

"Going Core" means practicing all ten—not just the ones you like. It also takes a substantial investment in yourself. On the flip side, you will discover that the people who invest in going core reach dramatically higher levels of success than those who don't. As a leader committed to professionalism and empowering others, you have a responsibility to go core yourself and create this culture throughout your organization.

Chapter Six:

Getting Started Fast

The number of people that dropout of Network Marketing early in their career is a lot! As I mentioned in Chapter 4, you make or break your new distributors in their first two weeks, and the first 48 hours are critical.

So this likely holds true for you as well...

If you get into action quickly and enjoy some small successes, you're likely to stay around. If you spend your first few weeks "getting ready to get ready," you'll probably end up doing nothing until you finally give up the ghost.

If you spend that time analyzing brochures, watching the company video one more time, thinking and talking about what you're going to do but never doing anything—the two weeks go by and nothing has really happened. Your excitement fades and your dream drifts farther away.

Now, if during your first two weeks you're learning the business, taking action steps, and actually getting people into your group, then momentum begins and your excitement level rises. Good work habits are created...which are rewarded with positive results... which motivate you to acquire more good work habits.

Please don't begin with the attitude that you will "try" the business. Come into it with the mindset that you will become of student of the profession and make a one-year commitment to becoming a professional. If you've read Malcolm Gladwell's great book *Outliers,* then you know that it takes 10,000 hours of experience to develop expertise in any occupation.

Now, in our profession it won't take you that long to realize a profit. But it will take that long to achieve true mastery. Like any new occupation, Network Marketing requires learning new skills.

The good news is you will "earn as you learn," but it's still a good idea to consider that first year a learning experience. For the average network marketer—working your business only ten to 15 hours a week—a one-year commitment is a realistic goal. I believe that if you follow this duplicable system for that time, you will be so pleased with the results that you will continue the business for the rest of your life.

Coming out of the gate fast!

So how do you get started fast? Avoid what happens 90 percent of the time:

You make a presentation and sponsor a new distributor. He's excited and dreaming of all the money, trips, cars, and other goodies he's going to get. He already has his first five distributors in his mind. So, you send him home and tell him to make a candidate list.

Since he already knows the five people he wants, he doesn't bother with the list, but instead just calls those five people to invite them to the next meeting. Then he sits back waiting for the big bucks to roll in.

You probably think you have a potential star in the making. But realistically, this new person has a lot of things working against him.

First, he probably made the invitations before he was ready to. He likely wasn't very compelling and the turnout at the meeting will be very poor.

Second, he didn't use a tool for the invitation, so even if he did a good job of extending the invitation, his approach will be harder to duplicate.

Motivation and positive thinking will carry a new distributor only so far. Unless he or she has a believable, logical plan for attaining his dreams, fear and procrastination will take over. And the same will hold true for you, too. So the purpose of this chapter is two-fold: to get you off to a fast start and teach you how to work with your new distributors so they get the most traction early as well. Here's my four-part formula for making that happen:

Part One...Build the Foundation (3 Steps)

The three things below should have already been done when you enrolled with your sponsor.

___Step 1: Enrollment Completed

This could have been done online, or you might have entered your information on a paper application and given it to your sponsor. As long as you have a distributor ID, this is done. This means you have locked a spot in the structure, and your position is assured.

___Step 2: Activation Order Placed

You must use the products or services personally

so you can get excited about them. How much should you order? Somewhere between what you need—and what will make you nervous. I say this only halfway in jest. You see, we've found that "just what you need" is not enough.

You'll need some inventory for loaning to new distributors while they wait for their first order to arrive, extras for temporarily out-of-stock items, and samples to give out with your follow-up packets. Make sure you have enough products on hand to build your business.

Some years back, I was working in a program that offered organic household cleaning products. One of the things I did with new distributors was to go through their house with them and remove all the "Brand X" products from their bathrooms and kitchens. We'd put all these in a shopping bag and give them to a worthy cause. Then we'd replace everything with the good stuff. This same concept will work for most programs.

___Step 3: Autoship Set Up

If your company has an autoship program, you should be set up on this for a regular monthly order. This ensures you never run out of product and are always qualified for any commissions and advancements you earn. It is the engine that keeps your business operating smoothly. It also allows the company to forecast demand to better ensure that products are in stock and available.

It is critical that you use the products or services yourself and can testify to how good they really are. Also, you always want to buy from your own store. You never want to ever have a "Brand X" product in your home that competes with a product from your company.

Don't think of this as an additional expense, because that is really not the case. Many of the products you use are actually "transfer buying" for items you would have paid retail for from stores. And depending on what your product line is, the long-term savings possibilities in other costs can be quite substantial. (Compare the cost of good-quality nutrition products with open heart surgery!)

Part Two...Get Connected (4 Steps)

___Step 1: Log in to Your Back Office

Go to your company's website and log in to your back office. Familiarize yourself with how to place orders, change autoship, and enroll new customers and distributors. If your sponsorship team has a website or newsletter, sign up here.

___Step 2: Learn the Company Policies

Set aside a few hours of quiet time (Sunday evenings are ideal for most people) to read your entire distributor kit. Learn which sections to go to for specific information and familiarize yourself with all the forms. Study the Policies & Procedures and Code of Ethics for your company.

___Step 3: Apply for a Business Credit Card and Checking Account

Having a separate credit card and checking account shows you are serious about conducting your business in a professional way and also provides a great way to track your business expenses. Your accountant or tax advisor will thank you later!

> **NOTE:** When you order products for your personal family use, buy them from your own business at retail. For example, let's suppose the wholesale price of one of your products is $25 and the suggested retail price is $40. You would write a $40 check from your personal account to your business account. Of course, you already paid $25 from your business account to your company. The $15 difference is really retail profit that should be credited to your business. Following this procedure helps you and your people appreciate the true value of your products.

___Step 4: Book Yourself for the Next Major Event

Most companies and organizations will have two to four major events taking place each year to help you grow your business. These events offer you information-dense training on the best ways to build your business. Some events, such as Leadership Conferences, are only for the higher rank team members, while others, such as the company convention, are for everyone to help them reach those higher ranks.

These major events are an opportunity for you to connect with the leaders in markets in which you may have some contacts and would love to have a group. So whether you want to build only in your home country or you want a business that spans the globe, you simply must get to these.

Frankly the people who attend these events have a serious head start on those who don't. They can cut months or even years off of your learning curve. You simply can't find any other substitute for being at these events live—talking to top producers and corporate executives personally, asking questions, networking during breaks, and immersing yourself in success programming with the best and brightest people in the your company.

These are the kinds of programs for which you would pay hundreds or even thousands of dollars, pounds, or Euros if you could find something like them in a public seminar. (Which you can't.) Find out from your sponsor when the next major event is and get registered now.

Part Three...Make Your Game Plan (5 Steps)

___Step 1: "Go Core"

The people who reach success in our profession are the ones who make commitments and stick to them. You learned the core qualities in Chapter 5. Now commit to them and put them into practice.

___Step 2: Set Your Goals

You must decide what your ultimate goal is from your networking business. Are you just interested in getting your products for free? Are you looking to make enough to cover your car payment? Or do you want to develop complete financial freedom? To reach your goals, you must first determine what they are—then set a timetable to reach them. This is your chance to make plans for the dreams you have.

Goals are dreams with a deadline. So write them down and make sure they are specific and measurable.

I believe that the average person, following a system, can achieve financial independence in this business during a two- to four-year time period. Think about what you want to do right away. Then, think about what you'd like your two- to four-year plan to be.

Dream-build with your spouse and your sponsor. Reawaken those wants and desires you used to have but probably lost somewhere along the way. Sometimes we get so busy in the bustle of everyday living that we lose sight of our dreams.

It's important that you discover your "burn." It's this burning desire that will keep you focused and motivated during the early development stages of your career when challenges are greater and the income hasn't caught up to your effort. This is the secret to staying self-motivated.

___Step 3: Buy a Daily Planner (Or Use an Online Version) and Schedule Your Time

The secret of rapid growth in our profession depends on how you spend the ten to 15 hours a week you have allocated for your business. You want to include as much real business-building activities as you can and minimize "busywork." Mark off the time when you will hold home meetings, make conference calls, and contact prospects. If you plan your ten to 15 hours a week ahead of time, you'll be much more productive.

Work closely with your sponsor to determine how to schedule your time for the first few weeks of your business. Find out the dates of all upcoming functions for the next 90 days so you can schedule them. Also, learn the dates of any annual conventions and conferences. These are major events critical to your success, and you want to make sure you can plan and arrange for travel and time off from work so you can attend them.

___Step 4: Order Your Business-Building Tools

As with any business, there are certain supplies that you will need to operate efficiently and effectively. You will succeed much more rapidly and better duplicate that success with your team if you utilize the proven tools your sponsorship line recommends.

These tools are designed to provide your prospect with authoritative and credible information about the products and business opportunity in a professional manner. By using these third-party tools, you do not have to be an expert to start having success. Just point to the tool and let it do its job. This allows anyone to conduct the business effectively—without special skills, talents, training, experience, or educational background. And using tools makes a huge difference in your ability to duplicate.

___Step Five: Complete Your Candidate List

This is one of the most important steps. Do not skip it and do not do it halfway. Just start writing down the names of everyone you know.

85

Try not to prejudge: *Well, he makes a lot of money. He won't be interested. She's a sales type. She wouldn't look at this,* etc. A mistake like that can cost you tens of thousands of dollars down the road. So, don't prejudge, just get down the names.

Out of every one hundred names, there will be three or four high pin rank executives, six or eight mid-range executives, and another 20 part-timers, along with some people who only want to use the products as a consumer. You don't know who's who...and the person who really takes hold of the business is often not who you initially think it will be.

Go through your address book and your holiday card list. Look through the business cards you've collected. Finally, skim through the yellow pages and scan all the occupations listed there as a reminder of people you know. Start with accountants, barbers, and contractors and don't stop until you get to x-ray technicians, yodelers, and zoologists.

Don't make the classic mistake of thinking of five or six people who will be interested and stopping there. You will certainly be disappointed. Make sure you get down at least a couple hundred names, so you can let people sort themselves into the right categories.

Now at this point many people will say they don't know that many people. Not true.

The average wedding has 500 people, 250 on each side—which makes sense, because the average funeral has 250 people sign the guest book. And this is not counting the dozens and dozens of casual acquaintances you know!

If you have a small list, this leads to weak posture with tentative or fear-based approaches. If you have a large list, you have strong posture, approaching people with strength and confidence.

Part Four...Blast Off!
(6 Steps)

You'll find that this section takes the most radical departure from earlier editions of this book. That's because once I developed this strategy of a "Major Blast," I built ten times faster than I had ever been able to do in the past. This is the most critical part of getting into action—and profit—quickly.

The concept of the blast is to expose as many people as you can to the opportunity using third-party tools as quickly as you can.

You do not need to be "selling" the products or opportunity. Let the tools do the talking. Remember, if your lips are moving, they should be directing someone to a tool. With each tool exposure, you should have a scheduled follow-up within 12 to 24 hours.

The goal of your Major Blast is to get at least 80 to 100 candidates into your prospecting funnel right away. Please understand that this doesn't mean you have to sponsor 80 or 100 people or even make that many presentations. Just that you have to give them an opportunity to look at the business to see if they are interested. It's important that you get a large number of people looking at the business to ensure you get enough business builders to get traction right away.

It may seem ironic, but it is actually easier to build the business fast than it is to build it slowly. When you start fast, you create excitement and momentum that spreads down your group. And by getting into a positive cash flow quickly, you set the tone for your team and create an exciting demonstration of success for prospects.

Network Marketing is perfect for everybody—but everybody is not perfect for Network Marketing. Some people are not looking for a business opportunity right now. Others want an opportunity but aren't willing to do the work. Yet others will become product customers but not do the business. It's all good. You just need to sort them out. The best approach is a multi-pronged one, creating lots of traction. Here's how to have a successful Major Blast...

___Step 1: PBR Blast

The foundation of recruiting is Private Business Receptions (PBRs). These are informal get-togethers at your home where you invite the key people you would like on your team to preview the opportunity. Ideally you want to have a video for the presentation or someone from your sponsorship line doing a presentation for you. It is a very friendly, non-threatening way for candidates to see what the business is all about.

Schedule your first three or four "Grand Opening" PBRs. Your first one should take place within three or four days of joining the business, followed by two or three more several days apart. Having a series like this will allow more of your prospects the flexibility to find a date that works for them. It also ensures that you enroll enough distributors to uncover a few serious people who will run with the business in a big way and create some initial traction for you.

Your goal is to complete at least three PBRs in your

first seven to ten days. This is the fastest way to create momentum. Here are some guidelines to conducting the most effective PBRs and getting started fast:

Prior to the PBR...

- Look over your prospect list to determine your best prospects and invite them to your home. Let them know you are having the "Grand Opening" of your new business and want them there to support you and see what it is all about. (These two words dramatically increase attendance, since almost everyone loves grand openings.)
- Don't get drawn into a lot of questions. If they ask, let them know the name of the company and that you have a special video presentation you want them to see or someone you want them to meet. Explain that you are brand new and can't provide all the answers yourself, but the presentation will provide the information they are seeking.
- Remove all distractions before presentation (phone, pets, children, etc.)
- Do not set up the furniture in the home for a meeting. Keep everything normal and move chairs in or around only as necessary when people arrive.
- Provide beverages only (no alcohol) or light snacks.
- Have packets prepared for each guest but keep them out of sight.
- Don't set up a product display.

The PBR itself...

- Welcome people as they arrive and seat them comfortably. Introduce guests to each other and start some friendly social conversation.
- Start within a few minutes of the scheduled time. Do not talk about people who are late or did not show. Concentrate on those who are there.
- To begin, welcome everyone officially and thank them for attending. Do a 30-second testimonial as to why you're in the business, then play the video or introduce the speaker.
- Don't be running around the house during the presentation. Stay seated and watch the presentation with your guests.
- If others arrive late, don't start over. Let them know that you will catch them up later privately.
- When the presentation finishes, hand out one info packet to each guest or couple.
- Now is the time to answer questions. If your sponsor is there or calling in, direct the questions to her. If she is not there, use the tools for answers. Example: If there are questions about the compensation plan, turn to the appropriate sections in the distributor kit. If there are product questions, use the product catalog.
- When you see someone is quite interested, ask if he gets it. If you get a positive response, then ask if he is ready to get started.
- Sign up those who are ready to get started.
- For those who do not sign up, invite them to review the info pack. Let them know that you

are building fast and want them to look over the materials promptly to make sure they capitalize on the opportunity. Schedule follow-up calls, or if there is another PBR or opportunity meeting coming up within a few days, invite them to that.

Following the PBR...

- Follow up with those who didn't sign up within 12 to 48 hours. Invite them again to another meeting or put them on a three-way call.
- Help your new team members schedule their own PBR series and start duplicating the process!

A few things to create a successful experience:

- Start on time and be brief.
- Don't over-talk the business. Let the tools do the work.
- Be professional and dress the part.
- Provide notepads and pens for your guests to write with.

Note: As you see, I still believe in the concept of home meetings. While there are many people trying to discredit them and suggesting that you can build the business by talking only to strangers, doing Pay Per Click advertising, or renting email lists, I'm not buying it. Those strategies don't duplicate long-term, and they are ridiculous in the sense that many of them actually suggest you shouldn't talk to your friends, neighbors, and acquaintances. If the people promoting these strategies really believed in our profession, they'd be talking to the people they care about.

Write out your timetable and plan for your PBR blast:

___

___**Step 2: Mass Market Prospecting Tool Blast**

You will want to get at least 50 of your mass market prospecting tool into the hands of prospects in your first ten days (average five per day). Not everyone will review it immediately of course, but you want to get at least 25-30 quality exposures from this—meaning people who actually take the time to look it over.

This step is best for people you don't think will come to your home for a PBR but still need to see the business. It is also very effective for casual acquaintances whom you don't know that well. It also works well for people who impress you as you go about your day-to-day life, whether it is a helpful retail clerk, a courteous taxi driver, or a personable waitress.

Here are some examples of what you can say to people you know. Look through these suggested approaches for one that feels right for you.

"Peter, the information contained on this DVD is the most important I have ever seen. When do you think you'll have a chance to watch it?"

"Peter, I know you are considered among the best at what you do. I believe you could be very successful in a new venture I'm involved in. I would like to hear your comments after you review this magazine. When do you think you'll have a chance to read it?"

"Peter, I'm launching a new business, looking for leaders, and I immediately thought of you. Please review this CD and let me know what you think."

"I'm putting together a group of the brightest people I know to launch a new business initiative. Your skill set is perfect for it. Would you take 30 minutes and review this DVD for me?"

"Peter, I have recently decided that I wanted to diversify my income, and I have launched a new business to accomplish that. My guess is that you will be more than intrigued with the info on this DVD. When do you think you'll have a chance to watch it?"

Follow Up...

You will have much more compliance with people reviewing the materials and a better response if you distribute them with a sense of urgency. Let your prospects know that you are moving very rapidly and ask for their commitment to review the materials quickly.

Use an energetic and busy approach, but don't go overboard trying to pressure the prospect. If people really don't seem interested in looking at the information, thank them for their time and move on. Your best results will come when you qualify your candidates and schedule a time to get back with them. Here's what that will look like:

After your prospect agrees to review the information, say, *"Great! When do you think you can see it for sure?"* Wait for her response. What time she gives you is unimportant. Then say, *"So, if I call you [right after the time she said she'd see it for sure], you'll have seen it for sure right?"* After she confirms this, ask for the best number to call her.

This way, the prospect has had several opportunities to say she'll watch it. By using this commitment approach (and if you have the proper posture), you will have an 80 percent or better compliance rate duplicated throughout your organization. Without it, you will have a much lower compliance rate, which will be duplicated throughout your organization.

When you follow up at the time you agreed you would, you simply ask, *"Did you have a chance to review the information?"*

If she tells you she has not reviewed the presentation yet, say something like *"It's really important. When do you think you could see it for sure?"* Wait for her answer and say, *"Great, so if I call you on _____, you'll have seen it for sure?"*

Just keep repeating this process until the person actually reviews the presentation or tells you she is not interested.

If she did watch it, ask her, *"Did you get it? Did it make sense to you?"* If she says yes, ask her, *"Are you ready to get started?"* If she says she isn't interested, thank her for her time and see if she is interested in becoming a product customer.

If the person is intrigued but not ready to go, escalate the process. This can be done by inviting her to a PBR or opportunity meeting, getting her on a three-way call, or asking her to listen in on a Leadership Training call or webcast.

Here are some examples of how to approach people you just met who impressed you:

> *"You know, you are too good doing what you do—to be doing what you do. I bet you would be amazing in my business. Can I leave you with some information for you to review? If it looks good to you, my number is on the back."*

> *"You know, I am very impressed at the job you do here. I believe you would be very successful in the business I am in. Can I leave you with some information for you to review? If it looks good to you, my number is on the back."*

"You know, I am very impressed at the job you do here. Are you familiar with Network Marketing? I'm in an emerging, new [expanding, established] company that is looking for leaders. Can I leave you with some information for you to review? If it looks good to you, my number is on the back."

Some of your best leaders may be people you don't know right now. So, as you go through your day, be on the lookout for sharp people. People who are successful in others areas usually are successful in Network Marketing too. Always have some of your prospecting tools in your car, purse, or briefcase for those times you come across them.

Write out your timetable and plan for your mass market prospecting tool blast:

_____

_____

_____

_____

_____

___**Step 3: Phone Blast**

This step works best for people with whom you have influence, who don't live close enough to get a packet to quickly, or who can't attend your PBR. Call them personally with a sense of urgency. You can say something like:

"Hey, David, grab a pen. Please write down this website: [website]. It's about a new business I'm launching, and I'd love your take on it. Please take a look, and I'll call you back at _____ to talk about it."

"Hi, Dave. I'm opening a hot new business and you're one of the first people I thought of. I believe you could do well with this. Have you got a pen? Please go to [website] and check this out. There's a way to earn free trips, a bonus car, and strong residual income. Take a look and I'll call you back at _____ to talk to you about it."

Always be sure to schedule a follow-up call for a specific time later that day or the next.

Write out your timetable and plan for your phone blast:

_____

_____

_____

_____

_____

___Step 4: Long Distance Blast

For this step, mail out at least ten information packs to candidates who live a long distance from you. Include a handwritten Post-it note saying something like *"URGENT: Please watch the DVD inside, look this over, and let me know what you think."*

This step works best for people you know but with whom you don't have a strong influence or haven't had close contact in a while. Often these are old schoolmates, former neighbors, and others on your holiday card list. For best results, give them a quick phone call and let them know you are sending them something important and when to expect it. (With the social networking sites like Classmates.com, Facebook, and Reunion, you can pretty much find anyone you've ever known in your life.)

Create a sense of anticipation on their part, then get off the phone quickly. Don't get drawn into a bunch of questions. Let them know you just have a minute and that the package will be there soon and explain everything. Also let them know you will be calling back to follow up. For best results, send their packages "Priority Mail" or whatever the equivalent manner is in your country.

Write out your timetable and plan for your long distance blast:

_____

_____

_____

_____

_____

___Step 5: Email Blast

This step is perfect for the people for whom you

have an email address but no physical address. It is also great for your prospects in other countries where sending packets is costly. It's a simple two-step qualifying process.

The first email ascertains whether they have any interest, and the second one directs them to a website or online presentation.

I did amazingly well with this process when I launched my business. It allowed me to spend time with the people who showed a genuine interest and not waste time with non-prospects. In the example below, you'll notice that I was right upfront that this was Network Marketing. If they had a problem with that, I didn't want to squander my time with them.

This is just an example. Work with your sponsorship line to create a template email that is specific for your company.

Message One...

SUBJECT LINE: Residual Income Biz

Hi Karen,

Are you interested in looking at a side business that can generate a very serious residual income? I'm launching something huge, and I'd love to have you on my team.

I am working with an emerging, new [established, reputable] network marketing company that meets the criteria to be the next billion-dollar company in the industry. This new company is a fast-growing business opportunity, and I'm looking for leaders in your area. We're trying to find people with good teaching and training skills who want to capitalize on a chance to get in early.

Here are the factors that make this such a powerful opportunity right now:

1) You can be in at the beginning!

The company has recently launched in [country]. So we have a real window of opportunity to get ahead in the race—before most people even know there is one. We're looking for leaders we can train in our team system to own their local market and then springboard from there.

2) Big Dollar Residual Income Available.

I'm sure you're aware how important is it to have residual income to create true wealth. With this business the compensation plan offers ___ ways to earn, with most of them residual.

3) The products are sexy and fill a huge market demand.

The products are _____. There are many lifestyle factors and trends that make these products in serious demand right now. This ensures you a stable business and income for many years to come.

So do you want to hear about this? Or are you too busy with your other stuff to look?

Please get back with me right away.

Thanks,
[Your Name]

Message Two...

Hi Karen,

Glad we had a chance to connect and that you're interested. I believe you can do great with this because of who you are.

We have set up a very simple system that anyone can duplicate. Please go to [website] and review the information. Then let's talk just as soon as you're done. We're moving fast right now, and I'd love to have you on my team.

Thanks,
[Your Name]

> **NOTE:** If you customize each message with a few personal comments, your response rate will be higher. <u>Also, these messages should be sent only to people that you know!</u> They won't work well with strangers, and you would be leaving yourself open to Spam regulations if you send it to rented lists.

Follow up 24 hours later for best results. If your prospect is interested but not ready to join, escalate the process. This can be done by sending him a packet in the mail, doing a 3-way call with someone in your sponsorship line, or sending him to a live meeting or webcast.

Write out your timetable and plan for your email blast:

_____

_____

_____

_____

_____

___**Step 6: Literature Drop Blast**

Drop off five to ten of your mass market recruiting tools at 20 different locations in your local market. Examples include the car wash, hairstyling salons, doctors' waiting rooms, hotel lobbies, coffee shops, etc. This will produce a lower yield than the above methods. But this method can bring you people you don't know yet and works for you around the clock.

Write out your timetable and plan for your drop blast:

_____

_____

_____

_____

_____

_____

General tips for maximum results from your Major Blast...

Remember the secret for creating wealth in this business is to follow the formula:

Lead a large group of people—to consistently take a few simple actions—over a sustained period of time.

Launching your business with a Major Blast as outlined above meets this formula perfectly. Anyone with any experience or education can follow these simple steps. And you will notice that all of these involve using third-party resources. This makes sure the business is not about you and that anyone can duplicate your results.

Always use third-party resources and don't try to make a presentation yourself. Be sure to schedule specific follow-up times when you give someone a tool. If they show any interest (even if it's just asking questions), then immediately escalate that person to another level.

The key to all of this is launching your Major Blast and getting a large group of people evaluating your business. As you go about it, maintain a strong posture. Be in a hurry. YOU have the gift. Don't ever beg. Don't be emotionally attached to the outcome with your prospects. If they don't like it, they're rejecting a third-party tool, not you.

Small Business Builders...

Before we move on, we need to address the issue of distributors who want to do the "small business." Small business distributors are not that interested in sponsoring others and duplicating. They are most excited about the products and want to concentrate on marketing them. They won't commit to going core or spending ten to 15 hours a week building their businesses. Their only desire is to use the products themselves and retail products to their friends and family.

They won't want the regular "fast start" training and won't do a Major Blast like this, so don't push them into one. Instead, with your small business distributors, simply spend an hour or two when you sign them up explaining where to find things in the distributor kit, how to order products, and going over any other procedural information they need to know. Give them an event schedule and emphasize they're always welcome, but don't pressure them to attend everything. Not everyone is interested in the big business. Assure them that you won't be pressuring them, but you're always available when they have questions or need help.

Do let them know, however, that it's likely they will encounter people who want to do the "big business" (sponsoring and duplicating). Advise them to bring these people to you. Big business builders are going to need help with presentations, training, counseling, and other things that their small business sponsors cannot give them. When you get a big business distributor under a small business distributor, you will work with the big business distributor as though he or she were on your first level.

> **NOTE:** When this happens, it would be wise for you to suggest that the small business sponsor may want to reconsider becoming a big business builder. Since the

small business sponsor is already doing most of the things required, by adding a few more presentations, he or she could upgrade to the big business and receive even greater rewards. Inevitably, small retailers will stumble across people who want to build a big business, and they will leave a lot of money on the table if they don't upgrade at some point. But don't push them. If they are happy to do the small business, be grateful for them and support their decision.

Chapter Seven:

Power Prospecting

Well, it happened again today. I got a message from a friend I haven't heard from in a couple years who wants to catch up. So I call him back and what does he really want? To ask me if I want to join his new MLM program. (Sigh.)

And you have to wonder...will these people ever learn?

I often ask these people if they don't remember that I am already in a network marketing company—the same one they were in and never did anything with. Inevitably they ask if I'm still in it.

"Um, yeah," I reply. "I made about $150,000 last month, so I'm kind of satisfied with it."

Then they usually sheepishly ask if I would give them the names and phone numbers of my friends or family who could buy their products. (Double sigh.)

It's much like the calls I get at my office. They tell Lornette that they have an urgent consulting or training project, and must speak to me right away. I call them back, only to hear something like, "Hi, Randy, my name is so-and-so. We met a few years ago at the MLMIA convention. (I've never been to an MLMIA Convention.) I'm working with XYZ Company, and I just wanted to touch base with you and blah, blah, blah..."

And it's always the same. The "consulting project" or "business venture" they want me to evaluate actually means they want me to sign up as a distributor on their front level.

Others will often say they are returning my call, or are old friends of mine from school (like I'd have any!), or tell some other outright lie to get past Lornette. They're worse than the damned toner and light bulb salesmen. They just don't get it.

So as you begin your Major Blast, here are some things to keep in mind throughout the process...

The people who make at least $25,000 a month in Network Marketing on a consistent basis never do irritating stuff such as badger or mislead prospects. They don't use dishonest or duplicitous means to reach people. They don't Spam people over the Internet, and they're not cold calling some idiots on a business opportunity list. They don't alienate everyone they know, and they aren't chasing "skinny rabbits." They are talking to qualified prospects and getting high-quality appointments to make high-quality presentations.

Sorting not selling...

Most people think Network Marketing is selling— and selling as getting the dumb prospect to buy something he doesn't need. So they devote their career to learning neuro-linguistic programming (NLP), closing strategies, and other manipulative techniques to coerce prospects into buying things they don't want or need. Anthony Robbins and a legion of little Tony wannabes have created an entire cottage industry teaching people to do this. Many MLMers have jumped into the fray, bringing these and other high-pressure sales techniques into Network Marketing.

These are the jackasses who call during your dinner hour, opening with lines like, "Hi, Jim, you don't know me—and it's just a shot in the dark—but I've heard you're a sharp individual, and I think you could qualify as an associate in a business I'm expanding." (Scream!)

A different approach...

I have no interest in trying to sell something to someone who doesn't want it, and I bet you don't either. Network Marketing done right is based on a simple, yet quite profound philosophy:

We're looking for people who are looking.

Put into more specific terms this means our job is to identify qualified prospects, then put our marketing message in front of them. We give them enough information so they can make the right decision for them.

If that means they join your opportunity or buy your product, great. If it means they don't, that's great too. Your job is not to *sell* your opportunity or products to those who don't need or desire them. It is to find the people who may *want* what you have and give them enough information so they can decide if getting that opportunity from you is a fair exchange of value.

Network Marketing is much more a sorting process than it is a selling process. It is this fundamental difference in philosophy that separates me from the multitudes of sales trainers, marketing gurus, and book authors out there. You don't need to manipulate or trick people into buying something they don't want or can't afford. There's no integrity in that.

One of the big challenges we face today is that so few MLM company executives understand the true nature of our business or the distinction between selling and marketing. So at every convention they bring in speakers to teach NLP, the three-foot rule, and hard closing techniques. If I have discovered anything in the business it is this:

> *The harder you close someone—the less he or she will duplicate.*

I'm a horrible salesman and have no desire to be a better one. I do take great pride, however, in being a great marketer.

The essence of our business is presenting our marketing message in the best, most effective manner possible—to qualified prospects. We give them enough information to make the best decision for them.

It is not unheard of for a schoolteacher or housewife to earn more money than salespeople in Network Marketing. That's because they can be duplicated much easier than a salesperson.

Now you're probably thinking, "Wait a minute, who sells this stuff?"

Good question. Obviously with approximately US$120 billion a year in revenue between all the MLM and direct selling companies, there are a lot of products going somewhere. But a lot of this is done without traditional methods of selling. It's done with duplication. Network Marketing is a business of conversational or viral marketing among friends and acquaintances.

A sales type may be able to go out and retail a lot

of product personally, but often he or she is not able to duplicate. That's because the non-sales types they approach fear selling and are often put off by the sales techniques employed on them. As a result, they do not get involved. But here's the reality...

Most sales in Network Marketing are accomplished without door-to-door or retail sales. Usually the products are conversationally marketed to friends and/ or family members and used personally. And because of computer and delivery technologies, most network marketing companies will drop-ship orders anywhere. It's just not necessary to stockpile large inventories and be delivering products all over town. You may be using the products personally and sharing them with a few friends and neighbors, who order direct from the main company.

Sales skills, techniques, and methods are great for sales. But remember that Network Marketing is really not so much a sales business as it is a business of teaching and training—a business of duplication. Using sales techniques—which work great on the used car lot—will often backfire in Network Marketing.

When sales types join your program and you have a system for them to follow, it actually prevents their sales skills from working against them. You and your people have greater security if you follow a system and a lot better shot at walk-away residual income.

Some network marketers appear to be succeeding based on their dogged determination, sales skills, and personal strength. They make a lot of money, and they look successful to their group.

But if they took a month off, their income would

immediately drop. If they took two months off, their check would be down 30 percent. If they took off three or four months, they wouldn't have a business to come back to.

When you build with a system, once you secure a line, you can walk away and it will continue to grow. You set the system in motion, and once it's in motion, it goes on without you. It's the consummate example of using the leveraging power of Network Marketing. But this works only when you follow the formula:

> *Lead a large group of people—to consistently do a few simple actions— over a sustained period of time.*

And if those actions are sales techniques, they probably won't qualify, because only 10 percent of the population are sales types.

So with all that in mind, let's look at what a solid prospecting pipeline will look like, so you can get the best duplication in your team.

One of the biggest mistakes beginners make is thinking that sponsoring is a one-shot, all-or-nothing event. Actually, it's a process that takes different amounts of time for different prospects. Your goal shouldn't be to sell or "close" anyone, but rather to simply give your prospects enough information so they can make the best decision for them.

Unlike sales, where often you are taught to manipulate or close people, in Network Marketing we are looking for people motivated enough to take action themselves. Some people are open to new concepts, while others are stuck with the preconceptions they've been taught. You're looking for the open-minded ones.

In his brilliant book *A Brief History of Time*, Professor Stephen Hawking opens with the story of a well-known scientist who gave a public lecture on astronomy. The scientist described how the moon orbits the earth, the earth orbits the sun, and how our solar system orbits around the center of the galaxy. When he finished, a little old lady got up and said, "What you have told us is rubbish. The world is really a flat plate supported on the back of a giant tortoise."

The scientist gave a knowing smile and replied, "What is the tortoise standing on?"

"You're very clever, young man, very clever," she replied. "But it's turtles all the way down!"

We all know people like that little old lady. The point is, why try to convince them otherwise? If they believe that the universe is a big stack of turtles—or that all network marketing opportunities are illegal pyramids—nothing you present to the contrary is going to change their belief.

It's not so much about convincing people or changing their beliefs as much as it is about finding the people who are open to what you have. It is a sorting process, divided into stages, where the prospect indicates his or her level of interest and commitment at the appropriate level. You will meet people who believe all network marketing opportunities are Ponzi schemes. Why spend all your time trying to convince them otherwise when there are legions of people who are open to what you have?

The truth is, resistance to Network Marketing is

crumbling as the profession continues to receive more and more credibility. Everyone knows someone who is successful in the business now, the mainstream media has covered the business extensively, and the old economic model has broken down. Network Marketing is regarded in high esteem in a lot of places these days. As it should be. So just introduce people into the pipeline, get them exposed to your opportunity, and let them sort themselves out.

The Ladder of Escalation...

The dynamic you want to accomplish is what I like to call a "ladder of escalation" We discussed in chapter four. Let's go into a little more specifics here. This means that each time your prospect moves a step through the pipeline, you escalate the process, making it a bigger deal than it was the step before. So here's an example of what this might look like. This is only a guideline. Check with your sponsorship line for the exact steps in your program.

The first step is going to depend on your relationship with the potential candidate. If she is a close friend or relative, you'll probably work with her differently than if she is a casual acquaintance you met standing in line at the movies.

As mentioned earlier, for people you know who live locally, inviting them to a private business reception (PBR) at your home is a great start. People with whom you have a relationship are much more likely to show up for this. For someone you don't know all that well, use your mass market prospecting tool first.

The tool establishes that you are in a legitimate

business, and if the person is a viable prospect, she may be open to come to a home presentation after she views that.

You may have people sign up at the home presentations, but don't worry if they don't. Many people will need a few exposures to the business before they sort things out.

At the end of your home presentations, ask people something like, "So do you get this?" If they do, ask if they are ready to get started. If not, escalate them up the ladder to the next step.

You'll send them home with the follow-up packet, making sure you've scheduled the next meeting, which is probably an opportunity meeting in a hotel.

Next the prospect goes to the larger meeting, which has hundreds of people in attendance. At this point, usually within 15 seconds of entering the room and estimating how many chairs are set up, she has made a subconscious decision to join. If not, she will most certainly join by the time the speaker finishes the presentation.

Understand this: Your prospect is desperately looking for a cause to believe in. Here's why.

We've lost our sense of community, even family. Most people miss this and are very much looking for something to replace it. They're looking for a cause, a movement, something bigger than themselves that they can be a part of.

To see hundreds of positive, proactive people together in a hotel ballroom—sharing an experience and having fun—is such an intoxicating experience for most people that they simply can't wait to join the team.

But if the prospect is still intrigued but not ready to pull the trigger, then you escalate the process again. This time you might put her on a national conference call or a worldwide webcast where there are thousands of people logged on. If that doesn't work, you can invite her to attend a major event, like the next regional training or even a convention.

The other dynamic occurring here is what psychologists would call "social proof." Every time the prospect sees the presentation, more people are involved, which creates a subconscious belief that the opportunity is building up steam, and most people are afraid of being left behind. And every time the group sizes increases, it seems like a safer decision, because that many other people have already made the decision.

In reality, most people will either join by the second or third look at the program or remove themselves from consideration. Of course, even when your prospect joins in the early stages, you still continue to move her along this process so she experiences the bigger meetings anyway. This just serves to reconfirm to her that she made a great decision and increases her already high enthusiasm.

This is a powerful way to build the business. The mass market recruiting tool feeds the home meetings, which feed the bigger hotel meetings, which feed the conference calls, webcasts, and major events. Every time your candidate sees the opportunity, it's a bigger deal than the time before.

It is very important that you keep the home meetings as part of the process. If not, you'll see that the large hotel meetings will lose steam and attendance will drop off. If distributors aren't doing the home meetings, it means they don't have a steady stream of prospects coming through the pipeline, so they aren't that motivated to get to the meetings themselves. Fewer people come, the meetings get smaller, fewer prospects sign, and the downward cycle continues. At the end of each step in the process, always schedule the next meeting. Every time the prospect sees a presentation, let it be a bigger event than the last. By structuring your recruiting process in this manner, you'll achieve the best possible results. Your prospect will get information in digestible doses, momentum will be created, and those who are real prospects will develop a sense of urgency.

Who really needs whom...

One of the biggest mistakes people make when they join the business is thinking *"Who can I sell this stuff to?"* This is completely off base—the opposite of what a successful distributor should be thinking. Here's the reality...

Every Monday morning at 6:00, 6:30, and 7:00 a.m., alarm clocks all around the world are going off. People are groggily hitting the snooze button, desperate for another five minutes of sleep. They get up at the last possible second, rush through their shower, then either microwave breakfast, skip it, or buy some crap through a drive-through window on the way to work.

We know that 80 percent of people are going to a job they don't like, or actually hate, and 99.9 percent of them think they should be making more money. Most of them will slog through the day in a comatose state and grab dinner at another drive-through window on the way home. Then, they will plop onto a sofa or recliner

117

and spend the night rubbing the hair off the back of their heads, drinking cans of rancid, fermented hops, watching mindless sitcoms until they're ready for bed.

Until Tuesday morning, when the process starts all over...

Till Wednesday morning..."Thank God it's hump day!"

Till Thursday morning...

Till "Thank God it's Friday!"

And you know what that means—it's payday. So, at five o'clock, when their boss whistles them over to fetch their meager pittance, they can feel—if for only a few brief moments—like the money is theirs.

Now, of course, that paycheck is already spent because they have a stack of credit card bills waiting for it. But for those few glorious moments, it feels like it's theirs. This calls for a celebration. This means tonight they can eat out! So at least here in America, that means off to Pizza Hut for a stuffed crust, meat-lovers, double-cheese, double-meat pan pizza, which of course they'll wash down with a Diet Pepsi, because they need to "watch their weight."

From dinner, it's off to the neighborhood video store or their online video rental, where they'll stack up six to eight videos—just enough to keep them from thinking about their life of quiet desperation all weekend. Until Monday morning, when the alarm clock goes off and they start the process all over again...

Do you want to know the truth? You don't need these people. Instead, it is they who desperately need and want what you have to offer. So stop thinking *"Whom can I get to do this?"* Start thinking *"To whom would I like to offer this opportunity?"*

You may think your product is vitamins, or skin care, or discount long distance service, but it is none of those things. What you really sell is *freedom.* Never lose sight of that.

You're offering people the opportunity to become their own boss and control their own destiny. For most of them, it will be the first opportunity they've ever had with unlimited income potential. It's also the first time they've had a chance to become successful by empowering others. Obviously, everyone would be interested in this, right?

No. Actually, many are not. Why?

Because it means getting out of their comfort zone. Because it takes a belief in oneself that they don't possess.

Some of them want success, but not if they have to do any work to get it. They're playing the odds, figuring a rich relative is going to die or that the next time the phone rings, it will be the Publisher's Clearing House Prize Patrol calling for their cross street. And many more think they want success—but are actually taking actions to prevent it, because they suffer from "lack" consciousness and don't even know it. (My book, *Why You're DUMB, SICK & BROKE... And How to Get SMART, HAPPY & RICH!* is devoted to this issue in its entirety.)

So, while the universe of people who need what you have is vast, the group who will seize the opportunity you're offering is much smaller. You have to discover the people who have a dream and are willing to do something about it (the prospects), and screen out those who are waiting to hit the lottery (the suspects).

The natural place to begin is with friends, neighbors,

and relatives. This makes the most sense, since you won't have to make cold calls or talk to strangers. People who know you will give you the benefit of the doubt and usually at least look at your information packet or attend your private business reception.

One of the things that concerns me is when new people say they don't want to talk to their warm market. Usually there's one of a few variables at work.

One is they simply don't believe the business will work. They say things like "I don't want to talk to anyone I know yet. I want to take ads and talk to strangers. Then, when I'm rich and successful, I'll go back to my friends."

Of course, this is craziness. If you really thought you had an opportunity that could bring you wealth, happiness, and fulfillment, wouldn't you be burning up the phone lines to tell your friends and family?

Or second, they are reluctant to talk to the people they know, fearing the *can't-be-a-prophet-in-your-own-home-town* syndrome. There is some truth to this. If you've been working alongside Joe for the past ten years, and now you come along with this opportunity to get wealthy, Joe is probably going to be a little skeptical. But that doesn't mean you shouldn't approach these people. You should. This is where using third-party tools are so important.

These new people need to be sponsored all over again so they really understand and believe in the business. And they need a tough-love sponsor who will guide them, even prod them into doing the things that are in their own best interests. Which is starting the business with the people they know.

These days I won't waste my time working with people who aren't willing to approach their warm market. When someone tells me that he is not willing to talk to people he knows, I refund his money and suggest he look for a new sponsor.

Now the final variable that can be at play here is that your new distributor has been an "MLM junkie," and she's already been to her warm market 20 times. She's simply too embarrassed to go back one more time. I can relate to this personally, since I went through exactly that.

But, I found a solution to this dilemma...

Whenever I am faced with a difficult challenge and there seems to be nowhere to turn, I do something that too few people do. In fact, most people think it's quite radical to even think about it. I tell the truth. Picture this phone call:

"Rod, this is Randy. You're never going to believe this—and you have every right in the world to hang up on me—but I've got to tell you something. I know we thought we were going to make money in that vitamin deal, and the bee pollen thing didn't work out, or the no-run-pantyhose deal tanked, and I know you still have those water filters I sold you—so like I said, you have every right in the world to hang up on me—but I honestly found something, and I think it's different. Here's why..."

Now, what if Rod hangs up? He's not a prospect. Remember, the worst thing that can possibly happen has already happened—Rod is not in your business! If you at least give him a call, you have an opportunity to change that.

Today I am a multi-millionaire. But if I would have been afraid to contact my warm market one more time, I'd still be making pizzas.

Truth be told, your prospect is really not likely to hang up. When you just tell the truth, and put it out there, most people will give you a listen. And there will be dozens more people on your list who have never joined any of the programs you ever worked. And you're meeting new people all the time. You met at least three to five new people this week. So it would be a mistake to just eliminate all your warm market people without even trying.

Meeting New People...

The reason most people in Network Marketing never make it to the director or breakaway level is because they don't know how to meet new people outside of their sphere of influence.

They have a short list, so they need a perfect invitation every time or they run out of people. Of course, when they only have a few people left on their list, there's a subconscious tendency to hoard those names for fear that once they've called all those people, they'll have no one left to talk to.

This is a self-fulfilling prophecy you want to avoid. So let's talk about how you can meet some new people on a consistent basis.

Here's your mantra:

"Two people a day brings freedom my way."

Think it and speak it every morning. Put it in a Post-it note on your mirror. Then just go out to live your life with the expectation of meeting new friends every day.

Start the day with two silver dollars in your left pocket. When you meet someone, move one to your right pocket. When you meet the second person, move the next coin over. You'll probably discover, as most people do, that you already meet new people every day. You just haven't been aware of it before because you just let the moment pass.

Now, instead of just acknowledging new people and moving on, practice the art of conversation. Don't try to sell them anything; don't approach them about your business. Just talk. Be their friend and get to know them. Here are some of my favorite questions:

"You from around here?" (These days, almost no one is from "here.")

"So, how did you get from _____ to here?"

"What kind of work do you do?"

"Is that a tough business/job?"

"What's the hardest part of that business/job?"

"Are you married?"

"Got a family?"

"So, what does someone do for fun around here?"

These questions get people talking about their favorite subject—themselves. Asking if they're from around here usually gets people going. Almost everyone you talk to is from somewhere else. When you ask them what brought them "here," invariably they tell you it was to take a job or be closer to family. Either way, that leads the conversation to family or what they do for a living—both fascinating lines of conversation to pursue.

Of course, when I ask if their business or job is a tough one, 98 percent of people tell me yes. When I ask what the toughest part is, in most cases their answers give me lots of good reasons why they should be in Network Marketing.

The key here is—you don't bring up the business at all. It's not appropriate, and it wouldn't be effective anyway. At this point, all you want to do is make new friends—two a day. This gives you more than 700 new friends a year! Now if you're meeting 700 people a year, doesn't it make sense that you'll find a few who are looking for an opportunity?

Of course you will. You'll know which ones by your conversations with them. Those who seem sharp and ambitious and express dissatisfaction with their job or business are your best prospects—the ones you'll want to approach later.

Maybe you're wondering how to get the phone number of the good prospects. I have a technique that makes this so simple you're going to be amazed. The most important thing is this: Never ask for a person's phone number. Most prospects get nervous at that question and don't want to give out the number. Instead, use my "magic" million-dollar question, the one that never fails.

Simply say, "You got a card?"

Instinctively they reach for a card and give it to you. And you'll be surprised; most will even write their home phone number on the card. Those who do not have business cards invariably let you know they don't have one—but then they'll pull out their cell phone to program in your number and then offer you theirs. If you're truly being a friend by just getting to know them and not trying to sell them anything, this happens a lot.

The main thing is to not go looking for people to sign up. Just go out and make friends. And remember your mantra: Two people a day brings freedom my way.

So now you're going out each day with the intention of meeting two new friends. As you do this, you're collecting cards and phone numbers. When you get home each day, add these people to your prospect list. When the lines you have are going down in depth, you can now open some new lines. So you look over your prospect list and decide who is the best of those prospects. For these casual acquaintances I recommend you contact them by phone. This allows you to be brief, get to the point, and control the situation better. The call should go something like this:

"Hey, Ray, this is Linda. You probably remember me; we met at the mall when you were buying a cell phone. You seemed like a sharp guy, and from our conversation, it seemed you might be open to taking a look at a business opportunity."

Usually at this point the person will ask what it is.

You respond with something like:

"I run a marketing business, and we're expanding here in the Dallas area. I can't promise you anything, but I'm looking for a couple of key people. If you're interested, I'd like to drop off an information packet for you. Then you can see if it looks like something you want to explore further."

The keys in this situation are: suggesting that he'll probably remember you and telling him you can't promise anything.

Because he remembers you, you were friendly, and it's a no-risk commitment, most people will be more than happy to review your packet. And because you're out there always meeting two people a day, you will never run out of qualified prospects.

Now if you still think you don't meet two new people a day, let's look at some places where you can meet good prospects.

First, we can rule out the places you won't meet them. You won't find them in nightclubs and bars. These places are for alcoholics. Go to places where people of higher consciousness gather.

Find a church that does lots of classes, like Unity or Science of Mind. Find some courses that appeal to you and sign up. People who take courses on prosperity, Tai Chi, meditation, and yoga are usually people seeking more, so they're great candidates for your business.

Also look at public seminars. It's a safe bet that the people who pay to go to a seminar conducted by Wayne Dyer, Deepak Chopra, or John Gray are looking for more out of life. Just be yourself, practice the art of conversation, and meet new friends.

And then there's my all-time "secret weapon." The number one best place to go to meet great people—all the time: The car wash. But not the put-eight-quarters-in-and-drive-through-so-they-can-break-off-your-antenna car wash. No, I'm talking about the hand car wash. You know who goes there? People with nice cars. Bentleys, Vipers, and Aston Martins, among others. People who have nice cars already know something about success. And the fact they take care of them tells you a lot about them. At the hand wash I go to, I've met numerous company executives (one who owns 47 Ferraris, a couple of Rolls Royces, and a few other cars), a Grammy-winning songwriter, two NBA stars, a minister of a church with three thousand Sunday worshipers, and a host of other serious people.

The secret to prospecting is having a long, never-ending list. When you practice the strategies we've just talked about, that's exactly what you'll have. Having that large list is the first half of the battle. The second half is how you approach the people on the list—your "invite."

Inviting...

Weak invitation skills can cost you $200,000 a year in lost income. Yet it's one of the most poorly taught areas of the business. Most people concentrate on learning a good presentation, or they figure they can always bring their prospect to a presentation by someone else. But what gets lost in all this is the fact that without a good invitation, your prospect will never see a presentation.

This is also one of the biggest causes of dropouts.

Because new distributors are not trained with good invitation skills, they blow off some of their best prospects. Not being able to even get their prospects in front of a third-party tool, these new distributors quickly get frustrated, and many call it quits before they ever get started. This is sad, because with the proper training, inviting is simple, effortless, and even fun.

This inviting is the most important part of your Major Blast. Whether you're inviting someone to review literature, come to a PBR, attend an opportunity meeting, or get on a conference call or webcast, the skill set is the same. Here are some general guidelines to help you.

Always make your invitation about the third-party resource and never about you. So you edify the resource:

Say things like "The information on this CD is so important…"; "The person giving the presentation is a multi-million-dollar producer…"; and "The people you'll hear on this conference call have made millions of dollars. They'll be revealing exactly how they built their business." This way it doesn't matter if you are brand new, haven't made any serious money yet, or haven't achieved a high rank.

When it comes to inviting, it's all about posture. You want to be firm, compelling, and fast. Don't let them drag you into questions. Keep referring them to the outcome you're looking for and assure them the answers will be provided there.

The other key is to make sure to always have some of your mass market prospecting tools handy when you're out in the world. This is when you will be meeting high-quality people, and often you will have only one shot with them. So if you have a tool handy, you have a chance. If not, you lose out.

When you're inviting people to your PBRs, there are a couple things that work extremely well. First is the concept of a "Grand Opening." For your first few PBRs, when you launch your Major Blast, let people know that you are having the Grand Opening of your business and you want them there to support you.

Imagine if you opened a restaurant or nightclub and you had a grand opening. Wouldn't all of your friends and family be there to cheer you on? Why make this business any different? Even if they say they have no interest in a business, tell them you want them there to support you. And if you want to really pull out the heavy artillery, use the second thing—a secret weapon I learned from my sponsor, Eric Worre. Tell them, "If you love me, you'll be there!"

At the end of the day, power prospecting comes from having a compelling invitation, directing the prospect to a third-party tool, and using the ladder of escalation. Let the process do its job and you'll end up with some serious business builders.

Chapter Eight:

Building Your Consumer Group

O f all the marketing strategies I teach, the way you acquire retail customers seems to be the most difficult for people to understand. That's because I suggest you do this the exact opposite way that most others teach. It's kind of ironic, but I want you to get your retail customers as a result of the people who choose not to do the business.

Most people teach to initially sell products to customers, and then try to upgrade them into the business. I'm very much against this approach for two reasons:

Reason one, it takes way too long.

With some of the products we have in this industry, it might take three or four months to acquire your "product experience," a story of the amazing results you got from the products. With this approach, it can take a distributor as long as a year to go down four levels. Whereas, if you lead with the business, it's common to reach that fourth level in a month.

Reason two, you will scare off some of your very best prospects.

That's because one of the reasons many people don't join the business is they think they'll have to go out and peddle products door to door. Obviously, that's not necessary, but they don't know that.

Here's what happens:

Let's say you work with Phil. And one day Phil is

complaining about how tired he gets every afternoon. Your eyes light up and you begin to lecture him on nutrition, vitamins, minerals, and herbs. After your 30-minute sermon on the benefits of healthy supplements, you introduce him to MEGA-POWER-ENERGY-BOOSTER, your company's special herbal formula.

Phil agrees to try a bottle, so you give him one and collect $40. Over the next several days or weeks, you talk him through using the product and monitor his progress. He thinks he's improving, so he gets another bottle from you when the first one runs out. You, of course, get another $40 from him.

A few days later, Phil comes back. "Eureka," he says. "This stuff really works. I have great energy every afternoon. My hair stopped hurting and my teeth don't itch any more!"

Now you figure you got him. He's had his *product experience*, so you can safely broach the subject of the business.

"Guess what?" you exclaim. "Did you know that you could get these products for free? Even (gasp) make money with them?"

"Wow!" Phil says. "How do I do that?"

"It's easy," you reply. "You just become a distributor."

"That sounds *very interesting,*" Phil responds. "But I think I'd rather just get them from you, because I don't know how to sell."

You're incredulous. "*Sell!* Whatever gave you the idea that you have to *sell?* We never SELL; we just SHARE."

Now, you can talk about SHARING all day long, but the fact is you SOLD Phil a bottle of

MEGA-POWER-ENERGY-BOOSTER for $40. Then you sold him another bottle and took another $40. You have unequivocally, without a doubt, proven to Phil that this is a sales business. So, if he's in the 90 percent of the population that are non-sales types, he won't be interested in the business.

When you lead with the products, you scare off the non-sales types—many of whom would be great for the business.

This is not to say that the practice of selling products first—then trying to upgrade customers to the business—doesn't work. It does to some extent, particularly if you are in one of the direct selling companies. But in this book we're more concerned with duplication and making the business work for more people.

The 10 percent of the population who are sales types will enthusiastically go out and market the products. And, even with the non-sales types, a certain percentage of them will be so impressed with the product results that they will get over their initial fear and reluctance and market the products. Most, however, will not. And for the ones that do, you will find this to be a long, delayed process.

They must try the products, experience some kind of "miracle" results, and then gradually learn how to market the products to others. This process can take months, even years. My experience is that people who build their business by leading with the products—meaning, retailing first—take five to ten years to build their businesses up to what I consider a livable income level. (If they even stay around that long.) On the other hand, distributors who use an approach based on the opportunity and follow the system like the one outlined in this book can do it in about two to four years.

Unfortunately, people are not as patient and willing to stick to commitments as they once were. If you follow the five- to ten-year program, you'll find that most of your promising people drop out before they achieve any success.

There are quite a few good reasons to have a large consumer group. First, of course, are the legal ones. Having retail customers is what prevents the program from becoming an illegal, closed system. Customers are one of the things that separate legitimate Network Marketing from pyramid schemes.

Another good reason is the extra income it generates for you. A great part of the population are not prospects for building a business. Depending on your product, a much larger percentage of people are candidates to be customers. You will buy at wholesale and provide it to your customer at retail. The difference is your retail profit. This profit will especially come in handy in the lean times during the first few months you are starting your business.

Another benefit of having retail customers is that they will often send you people who will become business-builders. The more happy customers you have out there, the more likely you are to get referrals.

And finally, your retail customers ensure that your personal volume and/or group volume requirements are always met, so you qualify for all the appropriate bonuses due you in your compensation plan.

So, we know there are lots of good reasons to have a consumer group. Now, let's talk about how to develop one and then how to manage it.

Let's go back to your initial approach and see how that is managed. Suppose you ask people your qualifying question, "Have you ever thought about opening your own business? Do you ever explore ways of increasing your annual income?" etc., and they respond negatively. They maintain they're happy with their job, and they're making what they are worth. (There really are a few of these rare creatures around.)

In this case, you would then go to what I call your "turn" question.

This is the question that turns the conversation from business to product. If you were in a nutrition program, for example, you might say something like "I ask because my business is helping people get healthy [lose weight]. Would you be interested in becoming healthier [burning off excess fat]?" Or, let's suppose you are in a discount long distance service program. Your turn question might go something like "I ask because my business is helping people lower their long distance phone bills. Would you be interested in slashing your phone bill by 40 percent?"

If the prospect responds negatively to both your approach question and your turn question, then he or she simply isn't a prospect for you. Now, if they respond positively to the turn question, this is where you present the information about your products (or make an appointment to do this as soon as possible). Of course, at this stage, you'd also present the prospect with the appropriate catalogs, product brochures, videos, or audios. By this process, you should be able to get a fair number of retail customers from the prospects who are not interested in building a business.

You can also pick up customers from the prospects who decide they are not interested in joining the business during the presentation and follow-up steps. You can increase the chances of this simply by making a certain statement in their first presentation. Say something to the effect of "And if you decide not to do this, we'd love to have you as a customer." By your planting this seed early, many of your prospects who decide they don't want to build a business will select the retail customer option. We'll look at how to facilitate this further when we get to the chapter on presentations.

Managing your consumer group...

Your goals are to keep your customers satisfied with superior service; to upgrade their usage through education; and to do this without taking away from the time needed to work with your business-builders. Ideally, you want to spend 95 percent of your efforts with your builders and manage your consumer group with the remaining 5 percent. Let's talk about some specifics.

One of the unique benefits you can offer your customers is exemplary customer service. Most everywhere they try to spend their money, they will be confronted with bored order-takers, preoccupied or indifferent clerks, uneducated service people, or downright rude employees. Show your customers you actually care about them. Take a few simple actions to comfort them, and they are likely to turn into customers for life.

Sending a thank-you note after receiving a customer's first order would be a nice start. If you are delivering the products yourself, open up each box or bottle and get the customer to use the products immediately. Go over the usage instructions completely and make sure your customer fully understands them. Don't leave until you answer every question he may have. If his products are being shipped from your company, arrange to drop over right after they arrive. If you cannot be there in person, be sure to phone.

There is much to be said about going to the customer's house and opening up the products and walking him through the usage instructions. You'll find if you don't do this, you'll have a much higher rate of returns. And when you go to pick up the products, you'll find a lot of people have never even opened the box!

There's bound to be some drop-off in excitement, or even buyer's remorse, if there's a lag time between the time a prospect orders and then receives his order. If you're over at his house reaffirming the benefits, showing him you care, and explaining how to get the best product results, you'll keep this to a minimum.

After fulfilling their initial order, stay in touch with your customers. Maintain accurate records of the business they do with you. If your company has an auto-ship option, get as many of your customers on this as possible. This ensures they have a steady supply of the products they like, prompt service, and that they will never run out.

If your company does not have an auto-ship program, it's your responsibility to call your customers and get their order. Don't expect customers to call you before they run out. Most won't. Then, once they get off your program, their results may suffer and you may lose them. By keeping good records, you should know when to call so you can get their order delivered to them before they run out.

Keep them advised of any specific offers and new product introductions. Suggest alternative or complementary products where appropriate. If any complaints come up, handle them immediately in a courteous manner. If refunds or exchanges are necessary, make them right away.

Even customers who are on the auto-ship program should get an occasional phone call from you just to ensure that everything is satisfactory. When you see relevant newspaper articles or items that would be of interest to your customers, send them a copy. If your company or sponsorship line puts out a newsletter for customers, send that to them, as well as any new product materials that become available.

When your company introduces new products, be sure to let your customers know. In certain cases, it may be appropriate to send them a sample. Check with your sponsorship line on this.

Let's deal with the question of inventory. Many of today's modern MLM companies have customer-direct programs that ship products directly to the customer and, in some cases, allow them to order direct via a toll-free number or website. This has greatly reduced the need to carry a large inventory. Nonetheless, you will still find it helpful to carry a modest inventory. This ensures you have product to compensate for occasional back orders and allows you to get new customers and distributors started on the products right away.

Good customer service leads you to your next goal—upgrading your customers' usage through education.

You'll find that the better educated your customers are, the more products or services they will use. This is where sending out samples, catalogs, newsletters, or new marketing materials comes into play.

You may find it useful to have a product seminar or open house in your area every so often. Your upline pin rank distributor should coordinate these events. Check with your sponsorship line on this.

> **NOTE:** These product workshops should be for customers and distributors only. You would not want to bring a brand new prospect who has not seen an opportunity presentation. This would be leading with the product, which would cause the many problems we discussed earlier.

From time to time, your retail customers may refer other people to you who are interested in your products or services. You will want to ask some qualifying questions to these referrals to ensure they are not interested in the business. This is because it's likely your customer did not tell them that a business option is even available. There are also two things you need to do for your original customer who made the referral:

1) Be sure to thank her for her thoughtfulness; and,
2) Be sure to again suggest she consider becoming a distributor. Make sure she understands that there is some referral override income available, and by not being a distributor, she will be passing this up. Don't pressure her, however. It

may be that she is still simply not interested in a business. Just remind her of the opportunity.

NOTE: Remember that this process we're discussing is for those doing the big business or duplication model, not for people doing the small business or retailing model. The small business retailers do lead with the product. I don't mean to denigrate these people by any means. You must appreciate every person in your network, regardless of the size of his or her business. But building a few hundred-dollars-a-month income retailing products is neither the focus nor intent of this book. I'm writing specifically on the strategies necessary to build a large network. Make no mistake. I want you to have retail customers, lots of them. It's just that I want you to get them from the people who don't become distributors.

Following the procedures in this chapter will ensure you a steady supply of new customers and a stable consumer base. Make it a goal to get at least ten retail customers as quickly as possible. Just don't confuse them with distributors. Sponsoring five people who want to be customers will not build a large network—only sponsoring business-builders will do this. You need business-builders and you need customers. Be grateful for both!

Chapter Nine:

Giving Powerful Presentations

By now you know that networking is a fabulous way to make a wonderful income, help the people you care about, and build residual income security. But all this will mean nothing if you can't convey this to your prospects. They are interested only in one thing: How Networking Marketing will benefit them. Establish this, and you will turn prospects into distributors.

You can talk about product research, company stability, and million-dollar sales all day long, but if you don't relate them in terms of benefits to your prospect—he's not interested.

You must lead with the *benefits*, then substantiate with *features*.

This sounds so simple that you probably think you already do that. The odds are that you don't. If you're like most distributors, you are talking entirely about features.

This means you tell people things like:

We're a debt free, ten-year-old company.
Our products are the best.
I made $2,000 my first month.
We have the strictest quality-control standards.
My sponsor is an expert in this.

If you think about it, you'll notice that all these phrases are about *you, your products,* or *your company.* That means they're *features.* Remember, we want to talk about *benefits,* and benefits are always about the prospect.

Five elements in successful presentations...

I believe there are five critical areas that need to be addressed in every presentation:

1) **Prospect benefits** (This is where you do the dream building.)
2) **How the money is made** (How Network Marketing works and why it's credible.)
3) **Company** (Why your company is the best fit for the prospect.)
4) **Product** (Why your products are good and what their market potential is.)
5) **The support structure** (The systems, training, and help you will provide the prospect.)

Let's look at each of them in turn:

There are some key benefits that you should mention in every presentation. They are:

- Unlimited income potential;
- Great tax advantages;
- Travel opportunities;
- The ability to choose the people you work with;
- Minimum start-up costs; and,

- The opportunity to become successful while you empower others.

This dream-building is probably the most critical point of any presentation. To understand why, it is worth a look at what causes people to make buying decisions.

Most people base their buying decisions on *emotion*, and justify them by *logic*. An example: After I got my first Dodge Viper, I was enraptured with its styling, performance, and the high I got from driving it. Since it was an RT/10 convertible, I decided to buy a hardtop version for the days it rained. Then I saw a yellow RT/10, and I wanted that one too. So I bought it. Since then, I've had a few more Vipers, an NSX, a Corvette, a Bentley Continental, an Aston Martin, and many other cars—more than I can remember.

Each time I told myself that all these sports cars were good investments, because they held their value well. Of course, that's just what I *told* myself. The reality was I wanted them purely for emotional reasons. I justified buying them with logic, but the logic was not the real reason I got them.

This is no different from people who vote for a political candidate because he "looks nice" or buy a car from a salesman they like. The woman who accepts a marriage proposal may think she's doing so because she believes her future husband will be a good provider and father, etc., but she won't really make that decision on those grounds. She will do it because of the passion, love, and excitement she feels for him.

Now apply this to Network Marketing. Most people who join will not do so because it looks like the sensible, logical way to build financial security for their future. They join because they want to be able to travel with friends, buy a big house, get new cars, receive recognition from their peers, and have a lot of fun doing it. For most of these people, these won't be new concepts, but things they dreamed about when they were younger.

Most of the people you prospect will have forgotten or given up on their dreams. To excite them about the business, you must reawaken these dreams. Probably no function is more important to the presentation than this dream-building. For many prospects, it will be the first time they've thought about their dreams in years. Once you rekindle this spark, you'll often find it results in a brush fire of excited expectations. And because your prospects are hearing about your opportunity at the same time they're seriously thinking about living their dreams again, they'll be motivated to action.

Here's an effective little activity I've woven into my presentations in the past. Near the beginning of your presentation, ask your prospects to think of five things they would like to *do*, *have*, or *become* if money were no object. After you've drawn the circles—or however you show the income potential—ask them if there's anything on their list they could have or do with the income you just showed them. Invariably there is.

This exercise helps them make a direct, emotional connection between the things they want and how they can get them in your business. Properly done, this can be a powerful tool during the dream-building segment in your presentation.

The other thing you must do in this first step is

to make sure your prospect realizes that the current economic model we're living under is broken. It doesn't work anymore, and any prospect who thinks it does is likely to end up poor and dependent. Some of the things I'd point out to them include:

- The distribution system of jobbers, wholesalers, middlemen, retailers and other parasites is wasteful and doesn't serve the consumer.
- Major corporations are laying off hundreds of thousands of employees.
- The secret to true financial independence is working for oneself.
- At least a million jobs a year are eliminated by technology, never to be replaced.
- Most jobs are built on working more hours to get more income—the trading-time-for-money trap.

You want to make a clear contrast between the futility of working in the broken economic system and the compelling benefits of this business. Here's the most important part...

Never attack your prospect's situation. This automatically closes the person's mind and makes him or her defensive.

Let's say you meet Jimmy at a party and ask him what he does for a living. He replies that he works for ABC Company. You say, "Oh, I bet that's tough. I hear they've laid off a bunch of people, their sales are down..."

He's going to go into defense mode, even if he hates his job. It's human nature. He'll reply, "Well, I haven't been laid off; my boss loves me. I'm a hard worker; they appreciate me..."

Now, on the other hand, suppose you say something like "Oh, ABC Company. That must be a great place to work."

He'll probably reply, "Great place! Are you kidding me? They just laid off 500 people, the benefits are being cut back, and I never know from day to day if I'll still have a job!"

You want your prospect to come to his own conclusion that his current job is not going to take him where he wants to go and that Network Marketing is his best bet. This doesn't necessarily have to happen in his first look at your program. In fact, it may be better if it gradually comes to him over the course of seeing the presentation a few times. (That's why the ladder of escalation works so well.)

We want to show him there's a better way and let him draw his own conclusions about his current plight of quiet desperation. If something's negative, use yourself as the example: "After 15 years with XYZ Company, I was downsized."

If something is positive, use the prospect as the example: "When you reach Gold Director rank, you'll get a new car for free."

This is also usually the point where you tell your own story—why you got involved. What you want to do here is lay out, in a compelling fashion, the factors that drove you to open your own network marketing business. I always talk about my life in the restaurant business, working 12 to 14 hours a day, six or seven days a week. Regardless of what field you're in, you can usually relate stories of a lifestyle controlled by your income and an income controlled by the time you spend working.

Most people start their careers at the bottom of the pay scale, and then pay their dues working for raises until they reach age 35 or 40. Around this time, they're at about the highest level they're going to reach in life. When they reach this zenith, they're still in debt and their spouse is probably working too. They're paying someone else to raise their kids and probably don't like what they do. If they own their own traditional business, more than likely, the business owns them.

To the extent your story mirrors this, share your experience in the presentation. By telling your story, many prospects will identify with your plight. This helps them make the connection with the next part of your presentation.

How you earn money...

This is the point to start drawing circles, doing the 5 x 5s, or presenting a simplified version of your marketing plan. Please note that I said "simplified." By this I mean a VERY simplified overview, not a two-hour recital of percentages, titles, and breakaway levels.

You have only two objectives in this step. First, you want to demonstrate how exponential growth unfolds. Your prospect needs to understand the general concept of how the business works, not all the specifics of your compensation plan.

And second, you want to show that Network Marketing is the means by which your prospect can get the lifestyle benefits you talked about when you were dream-building. As you explain how the money works in the business, you can tie it to the benefits he will receive.

I'm partial to "drawing the circles"—meaning I actually draw a diagram with a circle at the top, showing other circles branching off going down four or five levels. I have yet to see a more compelling, visual way to get the impact of exponential growth across to a prospect.

To make it more effective, write "YOU" in the top circle to denote the prospect. Then, of course, you continue the process, duplicating down a few levels more. Assign an average volume (a conservative estimate of the volume a distributor can actually produce) to each circle, and show the prospect how this grows exponentially. Then, at each stage, give the prospect a breakdown of the type of money he can earn by having an organization producing these volumes.

Designing the presentation to use is an exact science. ("You get six, who get six, who get four, who get two" vs. "you get six, who get five, who get four, who each get three" vs. any one of a dozen other possibilities.)

For most of you reading this book, your company or your sponsorship line has already determined this. For the few of you who are responsible for designing the presentation, here's what you need to know:

You may have to go through countless variables to get the right one, so be patient. What you are looking for is a sequence where the prospect in the "YOU" circle continues to move up in rank each time you add another level and also stays at least one rank ahead of the distributors on their first level.

I like to build the presentation so it takes the prospect to about a $100,000 or $200,000 a year income, plus a few perks (such as a free car or home or travel program if your company has these). I find this to be the most effective for the following reasons:

If you show massive incomes, like $50,000 or $100,000 a month, two things are going to happen. First, you're going to get into a lot of trouble with government regulators. Second, for a large number of prospects, you will have just lost their belief that this is something they can do. "Joe and Jane Lunchbucket," who've been earning $400 a week or less for the last decade, can't imagine in their wildest dreams pulling down a $50,000-a-month check. They'll just assume your program is for "other people" and begin to tune out the rest of your presentation.

If you show a $100,000- to 200,000-a-year part-time income, this is enticing to Joe Lunchbucket types because it is believable enough for them to put themselves in the picture. Meanwhile, the more sophisticated professional types will also be attracted...

They are smart enough to mentally continue the duplication process and imagine the possibilities. Even though they may be earning $250,000 a year, they are painfully aware of how much time they must trade for that money. They will be quick to figure out that they could replace that income in Network Marketing with a lot less time. More importantly, they will be enticed by the residual income possibilities.

As you construct your presentation, particularly the numbers, keep this formula in mind:

Your presentation has to be simple enough that your audience understands the concept—yet complicated enough that they are afraid to challenge it.

Do this and you probably have a good one. Now, let's go back to the sequence in your presentations. You'll notice I haven't included a segment defending Network Marketing or explaining that it's not a pyramid scheme. That's because I have found such explanations are no longer necessary. MLM has attained such credibility and positive publicity in recent years—and is so far superior to the old, broken economic model—I no longer bother.

Your company...

There are dozens of network marketing companies out there. Your prospect will want to know why your company is the best for him. Does your company have a free car plan, profit sharing, incentive trips to exotic locations, and the like? Lead with these types of benefits.

Use your company's visual aids, such as brochures, magazines, etc. Don't stress the features of your company—stress the benefits to your prospects. Instead of saying, *"We've had eight years of steady, stable growth,"* turn that information around to become a benefit: *"You'll be building a business with security. Our eight-year track record..."* Don't say, *"We spend thousands of dollars on four-color brochures."* Tell them, *"You will feel proud and build your business quicker working with our company, because of the first class, professional materials you have to work with."*

Just as you do in the overall presentation, you want to consider the features of working with your company and translate them into benefits to the prospect. Talk about conventions, newsletters, conference calls, regional training, and the other aspects of your company's distributor support services in terms of how they can help your prospect build his business.

The products...

The next thing you want to do is to show the value of your products. You may be accustomed to starting with your products at the beginning of the presentation. I think it's better to bring them in after you go through the benefits of the business first.

Your presentation should show the whole picture: products, lifestyle, and opportunity. This will make it easy for the prospect to decide where her interest is. If she is interested in simply being a customer, she will tell you so. But never prejudge anyone.

Now, you may be asking yourself, "How can anyone start the business without first having product experience?"

Easy. If you've done your presentation properly, your prospects will assume the products work as you describe them. They'll give you the benefit of the doubt. (This is another example of the advantage of working with your warm market.) And every reputable company I know has a 100 percent product satisfaction guarantee. Your prospect has nothing to lose and everything to gain.

It's ironic, but one of the main causes of slow growth in an organization is having too much product knowledge. Or, more specifically, assaulting a prospect with that knowledge. Distributors actually talk their way out of the business. It's just not necessary to update your prospect on every use, application, and result obtained on your product since Methuselah used the first one.

Does a car salesman demonstrate the side view mirrors, describe every part of the engine, and give a history of the auto industry since Henry Ford? Or does he simply let you test drive the car and see how you feel inside?

I see this "information overload" particularly rampant in the nutrition segment of the industry. Instead of giving business presentations, distributors are giving three-hour nutrition lectures. Prospects— overwhelmed by a vast quantity of facts, figures, and research delivered in one sitting—correctly determine they could probably never learn all that information.

Based upon this initial impression, they never seriously consider themselves able to do the business. The best you can hope for is a product customer. In this case, your desire to be thorough and professional is making you poor and lonely!

I believe the biggest challenge facing MLM today is that most MLM companies don't really understand the distinction between sales training and duplication. I encounter this often, especially when I'm asked to speak at company conventions.

Often, I've been hired by a company because sales are not increasing, even though their distributors have been trained by some of the world's foremost sales trainers. Of course, all these sales trainers have taught positive mental attitude, mirroring, modeling, closing techniques, and the three-foot rule. And, of course, being non-sales types, most distributors don't perform most of these actions, or the actions are not congruent when they do perform them. So, in either event, these procedures don't work for them.

This is not to say that most sales trainers are bad or that what they teach is not good. These tactics work in sales. But, of course, many of them don't duplicate in Network Marketing. This is usually the point where I'm brought in. My message is simply this:

Good marketing is just a case of identifying qualified prospects, then giving them the information they need to make the correct decision for themselves.

True marketing—with integrity—has nothing to do with closing, convincing, or "selling." *You must control the process. You must give the right information, and you must give it in manageable doses that the prospect can digest. But, ultimately, the prospect must determine whether your product, service, or opportunity is right for him.*

A presentation should be viewed in its proper context. It is simply one step (albeit a very important one) in this information-giving process.

Having said all that, let's go back to the product segment in your presentation...

When you talk about products, give a general overview of the product line or lines. Don't go into a detailed product-by-product description. We've seen distributors go into 75-minute descriptions of every individual product, their ingredients, where they come from, proper quantities to use, and what time to take them—then wonder why their prospect ended up in a coma.

Give an overview of your product lines, and then just pick one or two of your favorite products to talk about.

Here again, stress benefits to your prospect. Don't

just say, *"These products are unique and exclusive."* Say, *"These products are unique and exclusive, so your customers can get them only from you. That means you'll make residual income for years to come."*

If you're in a nutritional program...

Let's suppose that one of your favorite products is one that "cured" you of an "incurable" disease. If this is the case—please don't talk about it in your presentation! I know this may be difficult for you, but here's why:

Personally, I believe the great majority of maladies that send people to the doctor or hospital today are caused by their diets. Eighty or 90 percent of what we consume today is dead, processed food substitutes with few or no vitamins, minerals, enzymes, or fiber.

Ideally, the peristaltic action of your colon should pull your food through your digestive track, taking out the nutrients you need and excreting the rest. However, the reality for most people today is quite different. Each meal they eat pushes the putrid, rancid, decomposing food that is already blocked up inside their intestine. Because this digestive process is so backed up, many toxins leach through the intestinal wall and enter the bloodstream.

The resulting effects may begin with tiredness and lethargy and advance to yeast and other bacterial infections, auto toxicity, and even cancer. Who knows what other diseases stem from this breakdown in the digestive process and resulting toxins in the blood?

What we do know is that many people who join network marketing companies—and begin to simply supplement their diets with vitamins, minerals, fiber, or enzymes—experience such dramatic and immediate upturns in health that even so-called incurable diseases are vanquished.

But here's the sticky part:

You can't say that. The government has legions of regulators whose job is to protect the public from false cures and unsafe medical practices. These regulators have been glacially slow in adopting or accepting alternative and even natural health procedures. They will be quick to close down a company with distributors claiming to be cured of a disease. If you have had a miraculous cure of a supposedly incurable disease, leave that out of your presentation. Save that story for your company convention when there are no prospects—and no regulators—present. Just stick with the benefits that the average person experiences with your products.

How the prospect will be supported...

The final part of your presentation is where you show your prospect all the ways you will help her succeed. Let her know she's joining a winning team. Show all the training programs, meetings, sponsoring tools, and marketing materials available to train her. Tell her about the people in your sponsorship line and explain how they will be helping her build her business.

This is also the time to sell you. No matter how great your company and products look, unless your prospects see you as a benefit, they aren't going to be interested. Stress your personal commitment to their success and show them exactly how they could get started right now.

Every successful presentation will include all of

these five main elements. I don't think the order is critical—with the exception of the dream-building and benefits. If you don't begin with the benefits, it's unlikely you'll have your prospect's attention throughout the rest of the presentation.

Keep all these thoughts in mind as you or your sponsorship line design the standardized presentation for your program. Believe it or not, most people will not get involved with your program because your company uses an extra half ounce of this ingredient or travels to a distant mountain for that ingredient. People will get involved because they want a better lifestyle, and they believe they can attain it with you and your program.

Obviously, your company must be credible and the products must be good. I don't mean to denigrate those things, but people don't buy Ferraris because they have rack and pinion steering and radial tires. They buy them because they want to go fast and look cool. Looking cool is the benefit; the rack and pinion steering is the feature.

Do not take this to mean that your products (or services) are not important—they are critical to your long-term success. In order to have real success, you and your people must be product-centered. But this is done through use and education and takes place *after* the sponsoring process.

By presenting the opportunity with this approach, you will show the entire picture and give your prospect the information she needs to make the success decision. You can also bring in people who wouldn't otherwise give your program a second look. Show your prospect the benefits they will get, and you will have the constant benefit of new distributors in your network.

Other thoughts...

Here's another reality you will have to deal with. Most of the prospects you'll present to will have to do an Easter egg hunt to find the $500 to $1,500 cash it takes to get started in the business today. This includes the people with "good" jobs, supposedly making "good" salaries. The average person today is burdened with debt, living on 125 percent of their salary, and subsisting from paycheck to paycheck.

Most people will be hesitant to tell you this (particularly the ones with those "good" jobs). You will have to try to get a sense of whether this is a problem and work with those people. They might have to put their initial purchase on their credit card, wait until payday to get started, or buy their introductory materials in several stages.

But my advice is to never give away a distributor kit to help someone get started. As a rule, people with no investment in their business don't value it and don't approach it seriously. People who have to stretch and sacrifice a little to get started are much more likely to stay motivated and build a business.

That doesn't mean you should encourage them to go deeper into debt. But it might make sense for them to put their distributor kit and first order on their credit card, if they can get started now and make back the investment with some fast start bonuses and other initial products. I've started many a distributor who had fast start checks back before his or her first credit card bill had arrived.

While I don't believe in closing people, I do go into a presentation with the mindset that I have a business that can fulfill their wants, needs, and desires. I also make the assumption that they'll get it.

I have no compunction (and actually feel a responsibility) about guiding them to the next step. I may say something like "You know, you would be great for this business—here's the next step you need to take..." or "Hey, Doug, let's expose this program to some of the ambitious people you know. Then it might all come together for you."

I'm really not driving for either a yes or no if the prospect is not ready to make that decision. But if he's not ready, I want to move him further up the ladder of escalation. The further up the ladder your prospect gets, the more big events he is exposed to and the more educated he will become. As a result, he will discover that the business can help him solve his problems and live his dreams.

Let's go more deeply into this issue of not closing people. You don't want to hard-sell people, but you do want to make sure they get all the information they need to make the right decision for themselves.

Objections...

Don't necessarily buy a person's first response. A lot of people are hesitant to admit they're struggling and want others to think they're doing better than they really are.

Rather than ask why a prospect is not interested (and get his defenses up), I'll skim right over his objection and let him know that I think he needs more information. I might say something like "I'm sure you want to have all the facts before you make your decision."

Then, I'll go through the info pack I want to leave with him, describe what each item is and why it's important he review it. If your packet includes product samples, this would be the time to give them to the prospect and reiterate the benefits of using them.

If he will accept the packet, then you arrange one of two scenarios:

1) Set up a time within a couple of days to pick up the packet and answer any questions he will have. *"I know you're going to love these products. Jot down any questions you have and I'll be back on..."*

2) Edify the next step in a big way and get your prospect to commit to another meeting. *"You haven't seen this presentation until you've seen Dennis and Cindy do it. They've helped thousands of people all over the country be successful. You've just got to see them for yourself..."*

The best way to deal with objections is to answer them right in your presentation, before they even come up. When you see the same objections coming up over and over again, build them into your presentation. Here's an example:

One of the objections I saw come up a lot was people's belief that they didn't have time to start a business. It was a fear I initially had myself. But, of course, I had come to understand that if I didn't make time for two years—I would forever be out of time. So, I built that right into my presentation.

At some point in every presentation, I'd say something like *"When I first saw this business—dumb as I was—I thought I didn't have time to do it. Can you believe it? I was busy. Of course, I was busy being broke!"*

You can do this for virtually any objection that comes up often enough. *"At first I thought these products were expensive. Then, I figured the cost of..."*

By "clearing" most objections in the presentation, you won't have to deal with them in the follow-up process. This speeds up the prospecting and sponsoring sequence. I wish I could give you answers for all the objections you'll face, but obviously that is not possible. The variables will be different for every program. But, by counseling monthly with your sponsorship line, you'll learn the way to handle the most probable objections that come up for your particular program.

I don't suggest twisting people's arms to join. But you do want them to take an honest, open-minded look at the business. In some cases, you have to protect them from their own small-mindedness. You don't want them to have a knee-jerk reaction and disqualify your opportunity because they got front-loaded with water filters 15 years ago, or because their best friend has a barber whose brother-in-law lost $150 in the hot fiber cookie deal in 1994. Unless a prospect is determined not to learn the facts, I will always attempt to get her to at least review a packet so I can follow up later or get her further up the ladder.

If you have people who see the presentation but won't come for a second look and won't let you follow up, leave them on the back burner. Wait about six months, and then contact them again. You might bring the subject up again by saying something like "I just got a check from my marketing business. I need to know if you're serious or not about getting out of your job. I've got one night free this week, but after that, I'm pretty tied up..."

Other thoughts on your presentation:

I like to open mine by informing the prospects that what they are about to preview is a two- to four-year plan for building financial security in a business that's fun, rewarding, and empowers people. I advise them that to get this result, they need two things: ten to 15 hours a week and a dream.

This makes sure that they know the price. They're aware of the time commitment and this gives me an opening later when I'm ready to do dream-building.

Another important consideration is making sure you're prepared for success before you even begin the presentation. This means expecting a positive outcome and having the proper materials at hand.

Have a notepad and pen for all your prospects. Make sure you have the appropriate take-home or follow-up packets handy. (Don't give these out at the start or they'll be reading them instead of paying attention to the presentation. Keep them in your briefcase until the end.)

Take control of your own business. Even if you're new and your sponsor is handling the presentation, be responsible for bringing the supplies.

Dress and conduct yourself in a business-like way.

You and your spouse should show up looking like Mr. and Mrs. Success.

Remember that anyone you have to "sell" on your program is probably not the right person. We want to sort people, not sell them. You are looking for people who catch the vision. If they do, nothing is going to keep them out of your network.

But if they don't...all the cajoling, persuading, and arm-twisting in the world will not bring in those people as distributors. At best, you will have people who sponsor in just to get you off their back, and then leave the distributor kit in the closet to rot. At worst, you will alienate a good friend or family member. So, please don't fall prey to the misconception that slick presentations and persuasion techniques will build you a huge network. They won't. All those tactics will get you are dozens of frontline, inactive distributors.

Now, what if your prospect is not moved by the facts to join your program? Thank him and move on. If you've given someone all the information he needs to make a decision, and he makes one—respect that person and honor his decision. It will not serve any purpose to argue or try to manipulate him.

Concentrate instead on giving an honest presentation with genuine enthusiasm. OPEN people, don't CLOSE them, and you will be blessed with an ever-growing, profitable, and fun business.

If you follow this approach, you may find that initially you will sponsor fewer people. However, the people you do sponsor will actually do the business and, in the long run, you will have thousands more distributors in your group because of the increased duplication.

Now, let's look at the specifics of doing presentations during home and hotel meetings, and the differences between the two...

Chapter Ten:

Conducting Dynamic, Effective Meetings

L et's begin by understanding the only purpose of a meeting. Quite simply, it is to schedule the next meeting.

A meeting is judged a success not by whether product or a distributor kit was sold, but by whether another meeting was scheduled. At every stage of the prospecting and recruiting process, you should pull out your calendar at the conclusion and book the next meeting.

Give out an info pack, then make an appointment to get back together within 48 hours. When you pick up the pack and the prospect is interested, schedule a presentation.

Finish the presentation and give the prospect her take-home package. If she likes the idea but wants to think about it, schedule the "second-look" meeting.

If you bring someone to a second-look meeting and she seems even more interested but still she's not quite ready to sign, give her an additional follow-up packet and schedule when you will get back to her.

Only a fool makes a presentation and sits by the phone expecting the prospect to call back and join. At every stage of the process you must direct the prospect to what should happen next.

Meetings are a critical part of that process. A powerful recruiting meeting can determine whether you spend just another Tuesday night drawing circles—or go home with eager new distributors in your group. The preparations you make in advance are what will make that difference. Let's look at some of them.

For home meetings:

Before the meeting, check to see if you have fresh markers for the whiteboard (and make sure they're erasable). Put the whiteboard in the front of the room and away from the door, so that late arrivals will not be a distraction to the meeting. If there's a window behind the whiteboard, close the curtains for the same reason. If you're playing a video instead, make sure it's cued up; you want the TV positioned the same way.

For home meetings, make sure the children are away at the sitter's and pets are put away in the bedroom. I know you think your dog, cat, or pet llama is adorable, but your prospects may have allergies to them, and pets distract from the point of the meeting. Just before the meeting starts, unplug the phone and turn off your cell phone.

Make sure everyone you're expecting has clear, precise directions. "Turn at the green house, go down about a mile..." doesn't make it. Directions must be specific: "Turn right on Elm Street. Go three-tenths of a mile to the second light, which is Fleming Road, and turn right..." For the larger house meetings, it's a good idea to have someone out front directing traffic and showing people where to park.

For hotel meetings...

If the meeting is to be held in a public location,

selecting the site is important. Hotel meeting rooms are usually the best, because they are conveniently located, non-threatening, and have adequate parking and the facilities you need. Your hotel should be a mid-range to high-end property. Mandarin Oriental and Four Seasons are probably too pricey and parking may be $40. Marriott, Hilton, and Sheratons usually work well. Avoid downscale places like Howard Johnson's, Holiday Inns, and motels. Your prospect will judge your program by the caliber of the surroundings in which it is presented. Everything you present to the prospect should be professional.

Visit the hotel in person and look at your potential meeting room. Make sure the carpet, wallpaper, and decor are light and attractive. Avoid rooms with a baroque, dark mahogany-type decor. Make sure the ceiling is at least ten feet high or higher. It's tough to be grand in a low-ceiling room.

Check the parking rates, as high parking fees will discourage guests. Check the prices for microphones, screens, and other audio-visual materials you plan to use. Most hotels farm out these services to outside vendors, so they are not negotiable. Sometimes these costs are more than the room rent. In many cases, it's cheaper to buy your own. Some hotels, knowing you need a screen or a whiteboard, will charge you $150, even though they're built into the wall of the room.

What IS negotiable is the room rent. NEVER pay the price first quoted you. These prices are only for neophytes who don't know better. Let the hotel know that you will be renting rooms regularly. If the price quoted you is $400, tell them your budget is only $150, and ask what they have in that range. Often they will then find you a meeting room for about $200—the same room they were going to charge you $400 for.

Room setup...

If possible, put the lectern and/or whiteboard or screen on a raised platform. It gives the speaker more credibility and provides better visibility for the guests. Just as with the home meeting, make sure the lectern, board, or screen is at the opposite end of the room from the entry door, so late arrivals won't disrupt the meeting.

When I wrote the first edition of this book, I recommended having a large banner or sign with your company's name at the front of the room. I also suggested placing an attractive product display table and perhaps a "prosperity" table. (This is like the product table but features car brochures, pictures of local people winning awards, travel brochures, etc. If your company has award programs, such as a President's Club, etc., you would have those brochures on this table. The prosperity table can also be combined with the product display table.)

Now with the prosperity display, don't turn this into a full-time job. I started implementing them in my system, and I began to see the meetings getting grander and grander. It got to the point that each city I visited to do open meetings had a bigger, better setup than the last one. People were making photo boards, collages, and banners, hanging bunting and making the meeting rooms gorgeous. People were racing from work at 5 pm to have their rooms done by 8 o'clock. They stopped thinking about getting prospects there because they were concentrating so much on the room setup. So look for some balance here. We want a sharp room, but it's all about packing it with guests.

Other set-up notes...

Set chairs for only three-quarters of the people you expect. Have extras where they can be brought in quickly, but don't set them out. It looks very bad to have empty chairs. The fuller your room, the more likely it is that prospects will join. It's better to be in a smaller room with people standing around the walls than in a large room with empty seats.

Arrive early enough to thoroughly check all the audio-visual equipment. Have extra projector bulbs, etc., and check all the volume levels, including the microphone. One hour before meeting time, set the room thermostat to 65 degrees Fahrenheit. It needs to be this cool so that when the guests fill up the room, the temperature will remain bearable. If the room is not kept at a proper temperature, the meeting will suffer. The same can be said for lighting. Make sure the room is brightly lit.

Set up the registration table in the hallway, so that late arrivals won't disrupt your presentation. Encourage all distributors to wear company pins and achievement awards. Pick your friendliest, most positive people for the greeter, registration, and door positions.

Have upbeat music playing for 30 minutes prior to the meeting. Have uplifting music ready to start immediately at the conclusion of the meeting. Studies have shown that the right music increases consumer purchases as much as 15 percent.

Notice that up until now, we haven't even discussed the actual meeting! Because all of these things you do before the meeting are just as important as the meeting itself. Little things are everything!

Here's a checklist of the things you want to do at each meeting:

- Set the thermostat at 65 degrees one hour before the meeting.
- Test all audio-visual equipment.
- Make sure display tables are set up (if applicable).
- Start pre-meeting music 30 minutes before the meeting.
- Have tape cued for end-of-meeting music.
- Make sure meeting is posted in the lobby.
- Check for proper lighting.
- Have company banners, posters, etc., hanging in a prominent place (if applicable).
- Check microphone and volume level.
- Make sure product demonstration area is set up (if applicable).

The meeting itself...

Now, let's look at the content of the meeting. This is generally the same for both home and hotel meetings, with a few distinctions. Begin by starting on time. If your meeting is scheduled for 7:30 pm, it should start then but certainly no later than 7:35 pm. If you wait for late people, you will set a precedent, and you will have to start later and later every time. In reality, the people who are likely to sponsor in and do the business successfully are the ones who arrive at functions on time. Don't skew your presentation to the losers who are crying about the traffic and all the other reasons why they can't be on time.

The person introducing the main speaker should set the tone. This is just a friendly welcome and edification of the featured speaker. The purpose is to put the guests at ease, build anticipation, and set a positive tone. At some point during the first introductions, remind the people present to turn their cell phones and pagers to off or vibrate mode.

Now, we get into the meeting. This can be done in two ways—either by having only one powerhouse speaker or by having several. If you are having only one speaker, he or she must be DYNAMIC. Another option is to have three or four speakers cover different parts of the presentation. This is a nice way to format the meeting, because more people are involved and their varied styles and topics keep everyone's attention.

As for the meeting content, essentially you want to take the guests through the five key points we discussed in the presentation chapter.

1) Give them an idea of the lifestyle benefits available.
2) Show them that they can achieve these only through Network Marketing.
3) Demonstrate why your company is the best one for them.
4) Give them an overview of the product line.
5) Show them how smart and easy it is to get started NOW.

Your prospects are thinking, *"Is this thing for real?"*

and *"Can I do this?"* The emphasis of the presentation should always be on the benefits to the prospect and not on the speaker and company. When you explain the marketing plan, don't say, *"We pay 5 percent on this level,"* *" We have a car fund,"* etc. Make statements like *"Here's how you make money"* and *"Here's how you can win a free car."*

Finally, have the main speaker invite the guests to join, giving reasons for joining now and telling them exactly how to get started. They should also point out the senior distributors present, who will be available to answer any questions, and explain the literature packs you offer. Then hit the music, and go sign up your new distributors.

For home meetings, most of the variables we mentioned for content are the same. However, there are a few things you need to do differently. Let's look at them.

As the host of a home meeting, you should not be flitting around the house fixing things. You want to be sitting front and center, paying rapt attention to the speaker or video. If parking is a problem, have someone out front directing traffic. It isn't going to enhance your business to have a group of neighbors upset because you have lots of guests parking on their lawns or blocking their driveways. In fact, set a goal that for every meeting you conduct, home or hotel, you will leave the environment in better condition than when you found it.

If you have refreshments, keep them simple and save them until the end of the meeting. If your company has food products, these should be the refreshments. If your company doesn't have products appropriate for the meeting, offer some light, store-bought snacks, like chips or cookies. You never want to be serving home-baked pies or using fine china, because your guests will think they have to duplicate you.

Usually, you will have just one presenter at a home meeting. Either your sponsor will be conducting a meeting for you or you'll be presenting for one of your distributors. The proper introduction of the speaker is important to the success of the meeting. If you are introducing the speaker, there are four points you want to get across:

1) The speaker is successful.
2) The speaker will show the prospects how they can be successful.
3) The speaker is a friend of yours.
4) You're EXCITED!

Let's look at each one of these points:

If your guests know upfront that the speaker is successful in the very same business opportunity being offered to them, they will pay better attention.

Letting them know the speaker is there to show them how *they* too can be successful will increase your guests' interest and anticipation.

When you mention the speaker is a friend of yours, this edifies you in the mind of your prospects. They will feel honored at the chance to sponsor into your group, knowing you have a direct pipeline to the expert.

Finally, make sure they know that this is not something you're just thinking about, but a new venture about which you are very excited and committed to long-term. You might say something along the lines of "We are totally committed to building this business, and we want to share this opportunity with our best friends."

And just like the hotel meetings, you must politely remind them to turn off their cell phones and pagers. Pretty much the same process applies if you are playing a DVD or using another electronic presentation. Edify the speaker and content, then sit down to watch it with your prospects.

Now, let's back up and look a little more deeply at some of the critical factors.

Meetings should be fast-paced, intriguing, informational, professional, and FUN! I believe that the vast majority of your meetings should be done in people's homes. Personally, I like to see only two hotel meetings a month. One is held by the highest-ranking pin in your sponsorship line. It's a closed family meeting. Closed means that it's only attended by members of their organization (family) and their guests. Other lines in the area wouldn't attend or know about this meeting.

This gives the local pin rank distributor a chance to have a major event each month to support his or her group. These are usually much too big to be held in a person's home. It gives that pin rank's distributors a slightly larger event to bring a prospect to for a second or third look at the program.

The other monthly hotel meeting should be an open, cross-line meeting. All of the pin rank distributorships in the area would join together to create a major monthly event. With all the different lines feeding it, this meeting has a very large attendance and is quite impressive to the prospect.

However, in a launch environment, you may want to consider weekly hotel meetings. You can sustain momentum during launches with large weekly meetings and get some serious traction. The smaller home meetings feed the larger home meetings, which feed the hotel meetings, which feed the large cross-line meetings. Having this structure in place allows distributors to bring their prospects through the gradually escalating process we talked about in earlier chapters.

Here's the sequence:

- Mass market recruiting tool (for casual acquaintances)
- Home meeting
- Family meeting (this could be in a home or hotel, depending upon size)
- Open cross-line hotel meeting
- Major rallies, conventions, and events

Open meetings should be used only for a second look at the program. This ensures that there are only positive, qualified prospects in attendance, not someone who's just finding out that it's Network Marketing and which company it is.

Now, you probably noticed that a successful pin rank distributor conducts the larger hotel meetings. There are two reasons for this.

The first reason is how you control your system— by virtue of the meetings. *The most sacred position in your organization is whom you allow on the platform.*

The only people allowed are those who have already built a big business or people who are moving up in the process of building a big business. Here's why:

The people who speak at your meetings are being edified by doing so. You don't want to edify someone at the March meeting, only to have people hear that he quit and joined another opportunity in April. And if you have someone up on the platform speaking about things outside of the system, that will negatively influence your group. So, it's very important that the person speaking is someone who has built a group (or is currently doing so) using the system.

The second reason you have pin ranks conduct the open meetings is that they're good! To reach that rank, they've had to give thousands of presentations. They know how to get and keep a crowd's attention. They tell jokes, weave in stories, and usually tell their own personal stories of success.

I know a lot of people believe in weekly hotel meetings, but I am not a proponent of this. I believe they create a lot of codependent people who never learn the presentation, don't do their own home PBRs, and are always waiting for the next meeting. You'll also find that when meetings are conducted on a weekly basis, they lose their excitement and that sense of being an event. As a result, attendance will eventually drop off. *No matter how good a speaker is, if he or she does the meeting every week, people will get tired of listening to that person.* But, as I said, the weekly meetings can generate a lot of excitement in a launch environment.

It may sound strange, but you actually have to train your people how to go to meetings. Teach them that the real meetings are the ones that takes place before and after the regular meeting.

Before the meeting:

The only way you know for sure that a prospect is coming to the meeting is to pick him up. You can say something like *"If it's okay, I'll pick you up and we can talk on the way."* Arrive with your guest at the meeting 15 to 20 minutes early so you can get seats in the front rows. The closer a guest is to the speaker, the more the guest will be impacted. This also gives you a chance to introduce your guest around. Let him meet your sponsor, any other pin ranks in the room, and any other distributors with commonalities (same organization, same occupation, etc.). And definitely be sure to introduce him to that night's speaker. Now, instead of seeing the speaker as a stranger trying to sell him something, the prospect will be listening to what his new friend has to impart.

After the meeting:

After the meeting, you will want to keep the discussion centered on the business. Answer any questions the prospect has and see if he's ready to join. If not, explain the packet of materials you're sending home with him and schedule the next meeting.

Other things you'll have to teach your distributors about attending meetings:

- It is important to attend every meeting, whether or not they have a guest.
- Always be generous with applause and laughter.

- Business dress is appropriate. (If they claim their friends won't relate to business dress, explain that maybe that's why they need the business.)
- No food, gum, or drinks during the meeting.
- Participate if the speaker calls for it, particularly during the dream-building, as prospects may be very hesitant to get involved in this.
- If a handout is passed around, always take one, even if you've seen it before. (If you don't, guests will recognize that only guests are taking them. If there are a lot of distributors but few guests, they may feel singled out and become defensive.)
- Cell phones off, no texting.
- Teach spouses who are not presenting meetings that their role is very important. They need to be watching and listening to the crowd to see which prospects are the most excited and what their dreams are.

Let's look at how long meetings should be. Of course, this will depend upon what your standardized presentation is, but I'll give you an example of what I do, which will serve as a guide for you to follow.

Even though I follow the same standardized presentation outline for all meetings, my home meetings will take about 60 minutes, yet I will spend 90 minutes to two hours conducting a large hotel meeting. Here's why:

When I do a home meeting, I will conduct the full presentation. For a large-size hotel meeting, I will do the same presentation, but I'll go into more depth and add more jokes and stories.

When I do a large hotel meeting, I go to have FUN. It's going to be an event! The bigger the crowd, the more fun I'm going to have. I'll crack a lot of jokes about making money, taking vacations, flying first class, and getting rid of alarm clocks. In a large group environment, these things go over great. People think I'm an incorrigible rascal.

Now, were I to say those same things in a small, home meeting, they would come off as egotistical and self-centered. People would be looking at me thinking, *"Boy, is he ever full of himself."* Yet, in a large group, with the social pressures of others laughing and having a good time, they'll thoroughly enjoy it.

So the home and hotel presentations follow the same outline. There are just more jokes and stories in the longer one.

Before we leave this subject, let's deal with an issue that many people bring up. They claim that prospects are too skeptical, that meetings are outdated, and folks won't go to meetings any more.

Not true.

However, I will be the first to admit that if you walk up to the average person and ask her to meet you at a hotel on Tuesday night at 7:30, she's likely to run shrieking from your sight.

But that's not what you should be doing...

Remember, we said open meetings should be used only for a second or even third look at the program. It's true, the average person, invited cold, is not going to show up to an opportunity meeting in some hotel. But, if she is truly interested in your mass market recruiting tool, she will likely attend a PBR at your home. And, if she likes the first presentation enough, she will drive 40 miles in the dead of winter in sub-zero temperatures to learn more at a hotel meeting.

You never want to waste an open meeting. But the best way to get the prospect to attend one is to give her an earlier look at the opportunity.

If you do the early stages correctly, people will come to your meetings. And, when you do the kinds of meetings I suggest, people will actually look forward to attending. The monthly cross-line meetings become such major events that people get prospects into the pipeline just to bring them to the open meetings, knowing they're almost certain to sign up.

Meetings are extra work, and they take continuous effort. But the rewards are too powerful to ignore. It has become fashionable in the industry to advertise opportunities as "no meetings required." I believe in the old adage that you can find out what kind of a tree it is by the fruit it bears. Here's what I know. In the 60-plus-year history of Network Marketing, no company has ever hit—and prospered after—the exponential growth curve without holding public opportunity meetings.

Creating the meeting support structure in an area ensures maximum growth in that area. The home meetings feed the family meetings. And the family meetings feed the open, cross-line events. This pipeline ensures that there's always an upcoming timely chance for prospects to see the presentation again. And, each time, it is a bigger event, and the prospect receives more social proof that joining is the right thing to do.

Timing is very important. If your family meeting is the first Thursday of every month, schedule the cross-line meeting for the third Thursday. If your cross-line meeting is always held on the first Tuesday, schedule the family meeting for the third Tuesday. This ensures that there is never more than a two-week wait between a "big event" meeting that you can edify and bring a prospect to.

If you get a prospect into the pipeline, take him to a home meeting, and then make him wait three or four weeks for another look—you will likely lose him. His excitement will fade and he will move on to other things. Make sure this meeting pipeline is in place so there's always another stage for your prospect to move through.

Final thoughts on meetings...

Some distributors feel that it's the company's place to conduct and pay for meetings. This couldn't be further from the truth. Remember, this is your business and your bonus check. It is your responsibility to set up and hold meetings, and paying for them is just part of the normal cost of doing your business. If you allow guests to attend for free and each distributor pays a nominal cost, you can cover your expenses and have a great event to help your recruiting efforts.

The concept of holding meetings to generate interest in a business or product worked in 1970, it works today, and it'll still be working in 2025.

If you want the long-term security that comes from building depth, there's no better way than the properly structured meeting. Now, let's delve deeper into how you create lasting security as we explore *Building Depth...*

Chapter Eleven:

Building Depth

Why do some people build huge organizations and receive passive residual income for decades, while others work furiously to shore up and rebuild lines every few months? The difference comes from *building* lines versus *driving* lines.

People who build lines do it by the numbers. Their growth is based on duplicable actions that create more ongoing growth. People who drive lines do it with hype, and they must keep up that hype relentlessly or their dropouts are greater than their new enrollments each month.

Building Blocks...

When you build a line, you create a foundation and consistently build upon that foundation, creating a structure that will withstand challenges.

You build a line with the building blocks we've discussed so far—things like hosting PBRs and opportunity meetings, using third-party resources, and making sure that all of your strategies follow the formula for creating wealth. All decisions are made with respect to how they will be able to be duplicated ten, 50, or 100 levels deep.

Contrast that with driving a line...

You see this a lot from the "MLM Junkies" who are

constantly flitting from program to program, looking for their next sweetheart deal.

"Heavy-Hitter Harry" discovers many of his distributors are dropping out and his check is going down. (And the guaranteed income he received in his sweetheart deal is about to expire.) Naturally, he assumes the program has leveled out so he starts searching for the next "hot" one.

He starts spreading the word that he's available, and there will always be some gullible company owner who thinks if he brings on Harry, he'll roll over all of his team and instantly put the company on the map. Negotiations take place, a deal is struck, and payments are made.

Harry immediately takes out ads in the biz op rags or starts a direct mail campaign to get new recruits. His headline proclaims:

Find out why the Heavy Hitters are switching to ABC Company!

CATCH THE WAVE!!!
Call your downline now, before they call you!

Harry works the phone 12 or 14 hours a day, cutting across all time zones. It's a steady diet of rah-rah hype, promising spillover and getting in at the top. Applications are pouring in.

There are no real relationships developed, no building blocks in place, and no company or product loyalty. Ninety percent of the new people will never even place a second product order. Sales plateau, begin to go south, and then Harry starts the process all over again.

Even well-meaning people often resort to driving lines, although they're usually not aware of it. They don't understand duplication and are frustrated with their people's inability to grow. So they start sponsoring even more, stacking people under others in the hope of motivating them. They conduct voracious campaigns to drive volume at the end of the month, trying to qualify for the next rank. They may even ask people to stock up with extra orders to facilitate a rank advancement.

They probably have to make all the presentations, set up all the meetings, and do all of the trainings. They're the ultimate MLM "grinders," having to do everything for their team. If they ever slow down, things start to fall off.

The celebrity lead magnet...

I've lost count how many times I have seen this play out in the last 20 years. A company hires a famous spokesperson, and the spokesperson either joins as a distributor or actually starts up his or her own company.

All the other distributors are gaga over the massive effect this will have on recruiting. Usually this leads to major media campaigns inciting people to lock in a spot early because a steady stream of new people will be joining the company, based upon the halo effect of this celebrity. In the worst cases, this gets promoted with television commercials, and lead generation co-ops are created. Thousands of leads pour in. But what happens at the end of the day?

The celebrity doesn't have a clue about how the

business is actually built and usually doesn't even attempt to do the work it takes. In fact, the spokesperson has most likely been duped into believing that others will work the leads brought in by his or her "name," and that a nice residual income will be the result.

This doesn't follow the formula for creating wealth in the business and is antithetical to the process of duplication. The last time this worked successfully in the business is never.

Driving a line like this has nothing to do with building a long-term, multi-level marketing organization. But most people don't realize this. They just keep running on the hamster wheel until they finally burn out and quit. Then, they'll either give up on Network Marketing, believing it doesn't work, or they'll assume they didn't pick the right "hot" company. In either case, it's a tragedy. Most of this disappointment stems from this lack of understanding and training on how the business is truly done.

Back in the day, when old school guys like me started in the business, it was a simple equation to figure out how to secure lines and build depth. We were all working stair-step breakaway programs, and it was a simple process. Now with all of the Binary, Matrix, and hybrid plans out there, things are a little less clear. But at the end of the day, it's still about duplication and developing leaders.

Securing a line...

Back then, people would say that you don't leave a line until it's three to five levels deep or until the line breaks away. In fact, you should NEVER leave a line. Your role will change, however.

Initially, you will be involved in the day-to-day building of the line, working with your new enrollees in their fast start training, helping with initial presentations, and teaching them the fundamentals. From there, you will evolve into the counseling stage.

Now, you are out of the day-to-day building, but you play a much more important role—counseling with the leader of the line on a monthly basis. We'll discuss this counseling in more depth in the next chapter. For now, know that this is the stage when growth should really start to take off in that line.

Ultimately, the head of the line should evolve into a top-level pin rank themselves. At this point, ongoing counseling may or may not be necessary. You then evolve into more of a motivating presence for the line. You're the living example of someone who's "made it," and simply being who and where you are motivates people in the organization.

You will probably be the guest speaker once or twice each year at the cross-line meetings in their areas, and you may appear as a guest of honor at large family events conducted by these distributors.

You should always be supporting the line in one of these capacities. You will move from training to counseling when they have the fundamentals down, and from counseling to a motivating presence after the line is secure.

By secure, I mean the line is "cooked"—it provides true walk-away income. Even if you stop working with the line, it will continue to grow and provide passive income to you. This only happens when you have enough core leaders in that line.

The reason that most people fail in networking is

that they fail to identify and work with leaders. They are concerned with the number of people in their group or what their volume is, and they fail to key in on leaders. They are working only their pay levels, or, in many cases, with their personal enrollees.

To succeed at the high levels of MLM, you must identify and work with your leaders, regardless of what level they are on. In fact, a lot of the time when you are building depth, you will be working out of your pay range. This is the only true method to secure lines.

Working in depth (with the people sponsored at lower levels of your organization) builds security. Working in width (with personal enrollees) builds income. You need to do both to create a large passive income.

But you must secure first, then build. Use your counseling to secure the lines, then you can move more into the inspirational or motivational capacity. And when you have lines secured, you then have the option to stop working and reap your residual income or open new lines to expand your income.

Don't be deceived by high volumes or the number of distributors in a line. Big volumes and numbers are easily created by people driving lines. Make sure that your numbers are coming from the building-block fundamentals.

Lead by example...

Your number one obligation in the business is to become successful yourself. And then, of course, your number two obligation is to build success underneath your people. Most people get this mixed up.

The truth is you cannot show anyone how to attain

a pin rank until you attain that pin rank yourself. It doesn't work to think that if you just make a bunch of people successful, then you'll become successful. It sounds good; it looks good; but it just doesn't work. The reality is that you must become successful first. So concentrate on your own Major Blast initially, advance up the comp plan, and counsel people along the way. At each step you are modeling the behavior and showing them how the next level of success is attained.

Never do for a distributor something he is capable of doing himself. Your job is to work yourself out of a job.

Your goal should be to build your people up to at least a $5,000-a-year income as quickly as possible. This $5,000 a year is what I consider the break-even point for most distributorships. They'll need that much to buy their marketing materials, finance their self-development program, and attend the functions. Once you can get them to this level, it doesn't cost them anything to work the business, and any more they do from that point on will put them into profit. And because they are able to attend the functions and work on personal growth, the single most important dynamic in this process happens: They become leaders.

For the most part, you won't sponsor high pin ranks—you grow them from within.

Here's the process you're looking for…

Your new people start with ten to 15 hours a week. Work the fundamentals with them and get duplication taking place. Get them to break-even level as quickly as you can. They are attending the major events and at one of them, something magic will happen. They will get "over the line."

Something will click, and they'll suddenly get

it. They will make a decision that the business and company are the one for them, and they are in it until they win it. No matter what challenges they face, they will be there for the long haul. Their belief level is so strong that nothing will deter them, even though they may not be making a lot of money yet.

This new confidence and belief shows up in their recruiting efforts and the results they get from them. Their growth accelerates. Now, they're at the point where they earn as much working 15 hours a week in their network marketing business as they do working 50 or 60 hours in their regular job.

However, instead of telling them to retire, I will suggest they go up to another night a week so they will be out four, even five nights a week. I want them to do this until they get to the point where they pay off all their debts.

That's one of my goals for my new people—getting them out of debt as quickly as possible. So, I'm going to encourage them to stay with their jobs even after they've matched the income. This way they will double their income. They have their regular income at their job, plus they have that same income again from their network marketing business.

<u>Don't let people try to live out of the business too early</u>. Remember that most people are broke when they come into the program. So if they trade their $40,000-a-year job for their $40,000-a-year MLM business, they're still broke.

Encourage your team members to start paying down their credit cards, pay off their car loan, and make some investments in building their net worth.

After they are debt-free, except perhaps for their

mortgage, and making more than they ever did in their job, that's the time you can encourage them to quit their job and go full-time with the business.

Here's the exciting part...

What we consider full-time in the network marketing business is actually only about twenty-five hours a week. I believe that you can have a very healthy five-figure (or even six-figure) monthly income and never work more than twenty-five hours a week. Here's why.

The prime time for the business is evenings from 7:00 to 10:00 pm. Most people are working real jobs from Monday through Friday, so daytime is not very productive. The best times to work are Tuesday and Thursday nights from 7:00 to 10:00 pm. The latest you can start a meeting, by the way, is 8:00 pm, because it can take two hours. So that would go to 10:00 pm, which is about as late as you can do meetings.

So, Tuesday and Thursday nights are great nights. Wednesday nights are not quite as good because many people have church, but they are workable. Monday night is not quite as good because people have just gotten back to their workweek, but this night can work as well. Friday and Saturday nights are also not very good, because most people use them to go out and play. Sunday nights traditionally aren't good, but Saturday afternoons work quite well.

These suggested nights for meetings are only general guidelines. I have done meetings on Labor Day, and once even on New Year's Day. If someone has a big enough dream, he will find a way to get people there.

Generally, we've got four evenings and one afternoon that are really workable. Let's assume that your person is working three and a half hours a night for four evenings. That would be fourteen hours. Throw in another four hours on Saturday afternoon, and now they are up to eighteen. That leaves them seven hours a week where they might be prospecting if they are looking for future lines; taking care of minor paper work; and using the rest of the time to counsel their leaders. So, assuming they are working with three or four lines, which is about the most I would recommend for anyone at one time, they would be working at the most twenty-five hours.

The rest of the time during the week, the best thing they can do is live the lifestyle. Wake up at the crack of noon; sit on their balcony as I do drinking my herbal tea watching the sailboats bobbing in the water. Go out to lunch or dinner, go shopping, play tennis, visit friends, do some volunteer work, or maybe for the first time ever, go to their kids' after-school soccer games. Just live the lifestyle.

This does two things. One, simply living the lifestyle tremendously motivates the people in your organization because they would like to have that lifestyle. And living well will also attract a number of very good prospects to you, because they look at the lifestyle, harmony, and balance you've achieved and want it too. You really do start to attract more and more people to you. The longer you're in the business, the easier it becomes.

When you work this process with a line, you can build it up to a high-level pin rank within a two- to four-year period. And the people in your organization will be earning more money than they ever have before, so they will likely never leave. That's a secure line. Do this a couple times and you have a nice income. Do it six or eight times, and you'll be one of the wealthiest people in the world and live a lifestyle most will envy. Now, let's look at the leadership strategies you'll need once that happens...

Chapter Twelve:

Creating a Leadership Factory in Your Group

A few years back I was asked to submit a chapter to a book on leadership, explaining how I would define it. My definition was:

Leadership is the ability to lead people to willingly do things they wouldn't ordinarily want to do.

In the military environment, a leader might inspire troops to get out of a foxhole and charge an enemy encampment. In a corporate environment, a leader may empower an employee to take immediate action to save an important account. A leader in a network marketing organization might inspire someone to overcome her fear and speak in front of a group or simply cause a new distributor to buy his first suit or tie.

In each case, the person wouldn't normally want to take these actions but willingly did them anyway—specifically because of the leadership influence of his or her leader.

I believe this is possible because of the increase in belief and esteem the people have achieved as a result of their exposure to that leader. The leader has done much more than demonstrate leadership skills and qualities—he or she has helped develop positive growth in the individuals they lead.

Leaders are able to do this by helping those who follow them believe in themselves and teaching them not *what* to think but *how* to think.

The old leadership model was to teach people what to think. In the military model, examples of this would be secret police, the many civilian massacres, and the Third Reich. The belief was that you simply indoctrinate in people what to think (and one of those thoughts is to never question authority) and they will follow. These examples demonstrate the negative potential of leadership.

Unfortunately, most people today are actively looking to be shown what to think. They search the globe for gurus to follow and movements to join. The strong growth today of gangs, religions, and cults is a manifestation of this.

People watch ESPN and other sports programs to learn what they should think about their local quarterback; they listen to bombastic buffoons on talk-radio stations to know what to think about political issues; they read the social columns so they can know who or what is hip, hot, and trendy. The education system around the world is moving from institutions that teach people how to think into places that disseminate facts to memorize.

Although this environment exists, real leaders do not exploit it. They carefully choose the people they lead and select only those who are interested in thinking for themselves. They create situations where people develop problem-solving skills, which fosters thought and builds belief in themselves.

True leaders don't develop people's belief in the leader; they develop a belief *in the follower*.

Leaders foster growing confidence and esteem in those who follow them. They help their followers think independently. This freethinking and newfound confidence causes followers to empower themselves into leadership ways of their own. Leaders beget more leaders, the real test of leadership.

I've said the biggest cause of failure for most people in Network Marketing is their failure to identify and work with the leaders in their organization. By the same token, you need to identify and work with the leaders up in your sponsorship line. They are your best source of help. When you create partnerships with the leaders in your sponsorship line, you demonstrate the leadership traits that will develop more leaders in your group, as they will duplicate the same process down the group. Your goal is to create a "leadership factory," where each month a whole new crop of leaders are making their way up the compensation plan.

Probably the most important leadership role you will play is modeling the proper behavior for your team to emulate. And this can be done best if you teach them the business as you—and they—are doing it.

Demonstrate the proper actions and get your people to *study, do,* and *teach*, all simultaneously. Instead of doing training sessions on how to do home meetings, get in your new distributor's living room and hold meetings for him. Don't train your people on three-ways calls, do three-way calls with them.

Monthly counseling...

This is the monthly process you go through with the leaders and potential leaders in your organization to keep them growing on a consistent basis. Here's how counseling works.

Let's say you're a Bronze Director with your company and the next rank up is Silver Director. You would counsel with the first Silver Director in your sponsorship line. Now, once you become a Silver Director, if your sponsor is still a Silver Director, you would no longer counsel with her. You would go, instead, to her sponsor, who is a Gold Director. (As we discussed earlier, if you want to know how to be a Gold Director, you have to talk to somebody who has already done it. If you want to be a Diamond Director, you need to be counseled by a Diamond Director.) You should counsel with the upline person at the next rank above you.

This ensures everyone has someone to counsel with, and also that the top ranks don't have thousands of people looking to them for counseling. Just like the sponsorship lines work, you work with your frontline leaders, who work with their frontline leaders, who work with their frontline leaders. In the event you're in a sponsorship line with a level or two at the same rank as you, go up the organization and you will find someone who will be willing to work with you.

It should be noted that just because your sponsor is the same rank as you does not mean that she is a bad leader or doesn't know the business. It may just mean that she's helped you achieve fast growth.

What quite often happens is that sponsors bring

people up to their own rank slightly before they've moved up a rank themselves. So, don't judge her or hold that against her. Celebrate the fact that she's helped you get this far and counsel with the appropriate person in your sponsorship line. Your job is to learn from that person's experience. He will already have made the same mistakes that you are headed towards, which means he can cut many years off your learning curve. Be open-minded and coachable, for he has a vested interest in your success.

Counseling can only help you, however, if you do a real one. The person to whom you go for counseling needs real information to work with. Don't draw out twelve lines if you really have only two active, core lines. Otherwise, the counseling is a sham, and the advice you receive won't really help you.

Now, let's look at how to do the actual counseling. We collect the relevant information we need. (You'll find samples of generic counseling forms in my *Duplication Nation* training program.) When you counsel someone, you need to know his rank, how many distributors are in his group, how many lines he has, what his average volume is, and a number of other variables.

Leadership stats...

Probably two of the most important variables you should be concerned with are the number of lines with a leader and the total number of leaders in the organization. To me, these are the two most critical statistics that determine all future growth. We know that a line could have fifteen people in it—but if none of them are leaders, within three months, the line will probably have diminished to one or two people or be gone entirely.

Another line might have only two people in it, but if they're both leaders, that line may grow to forty or fifty a month later. Leaders produce leaders. So that's the number one factor you want to watch for when you are counseling—the leaders in the organization.

Leaders follow as well...

The last leadership issue we need to revisit is the importance of honoring and following the system in your organization. Great leaders know that there is also a time to follow.

Because leaders are strong-minded, this can be a challenge. But the system must remain sacred with you as a leader. If you change the system, even only slightly, you will send a message to the organization that it's okay to change the system. Then the next level does it, and by four levels down, the system no longer exists.

Of course, from time to time, market conditions will dictate that you should change the system. Let me give you an idea of how you might go about that if you need to do so...

Let's say you have reached the top-rank pin level in your company, and you have five top-rank pin levels on your frontline, and you're thinking about changing something in your system. Suppose you want to take out a book that you're currently using at one part of the sponsoring process and substitute another in its place. I would bring that up at your annual Leadership Conference or at another event your top leaders would attend, which occur from time to time.

In my case, the event was what we called a "Diamond Weekend." Because it was not an official company event, each Diamond distributorship paid its own way. This brief getaway gave the Diamonds a chance to get together on an informal basis to talk shop. Before the weekend took place, we would each send out a copy of the new book we were proposing to every one of the attendees and ask them to read it. Then when we got together, we discussed each book and a decision would be made and a date set for it to be implemented.

This is the only way the system can be changed—from the inside as an entire organization. When you effect change in that way, it protects the integrity of the system. Then the system protects the integrity of your residual income.

Now, let's look at how to diversify that residual income by sponsoring long distance lines...

Chapter Thirteen:

Building Long Distance Lines

One of the first things your new distributors are likely to ask you is *"Hey, when are you going to have meetings in XYZ city? I know lots of people there."* This is an escapist mentality. Instead of building their businesses locally, which they can actively do right now, they're fantasizing about a faraway city, because that gives them a chance to procrastinate.

Here's wha t you need to know and make sure each of your people knows. Your local lines should be your primary sources of income. You must have a strong, sound, local organization that grows on a continuous basis, and you should always begin locally.

This is the easiest, most cost-effective way to build. As you begin to develop depth, lines will start to expand into other states. By the time you get down seven or eight levels, it will not be unusual for you to be in eight or ten different states or provinces. But, first you must develop a strong, local foundation.

Now before we go further, let me clarify what I mean by a long distance line. If you can get off work at 5 pm, drive to your venue, and arrive in time to start a meeting at 8 pm, that is a *local* line! I realize this is time-consuming and inconvenient, but this line can really still be handled in the same manner as your other local lines.

There are lots of good reasons to build long distance, but there are also some drawbacks if it's not done correctly. Let's talk about that.

Some of the reasons you want to sponsor long distance lines include overzealous government regulators, negative publicity, economic conditions, loss of key people, and natural disasters. All of these things are factors that can dramatically affect your income if it is all tied up in one local group.

Let's suppose you have an overzealous attorney general who wants to run for governor, and he's looking for some free publicity. He figures the best way is get that is to take on one of those evil, greedy, predatory MLM companies, and he picks yours. So, he's holding press conferences every day for two weeks as he attacks your company.

What do you think that would do to your income if he got air time on the late news every night? The same thing can happen if the local newspaper does an investigative journalism series with the slant that Network Marketing is a rip-off, and your company is on the front page of the local news section every day for two weeks.

If your whole line is local and all tied under one or two people, where will you be if they should leave for another opportunity? What about if a natural disaster strikes? Here in South Florida, where I live in the winter, we saw massive attrition that took years to rebuild after Hurricane Andrew struck. All of these things are very good reasons to protect yourself and diversify your income by sponsoring long distance.

There are some other benefits, as well. If you're

like me and enjoy traveling, you'll like having groups around the country (or the world) in beautiful destinations. Long distance sponsoring is a wonderful way to finance your travel and get great tax breaks. It allows you to see some beautiful cities and countries, developing new friends along the way. If your company has an aggressive international presence, you can develop a business on which the sun never sets.

Now, some of the drawbacks.

First, of course, it costs more money. Take a prospect to an open meeting in your town, and it will cost you only a nominal amount. Fly 1,500 miles to spend a weekend with a new line, and you can easily spend $1,000. For that reason, you need to have a solid, local group first. You can use the income from your local lines to invest in developing long distance lines.

This is also one of the reasons why I don't encourage people to quit their jobs right away. Most people want to do this as soon as they are making a few thousand dollars a month. Instead of trying to live on their newfound income, however, they are much better served by keeping their job and using their bonus check to invest in long distance lines. The long distance lines do require more investment, but they are well worth it, since they give you both more income and security.

Another drawback of working with long distance lines is that you cannot be there to look your distributors in the eye on a day-to-day basis when they encounter challenges or celebrate victories. But phone service is very cheap now, voice-over Internet is available, and there are numerous chat programs. And if you have a Mac, then their iChat even lets you see each other while you are chatting. So this is becoming less and less of an issue.

And there is another, very big hidden benefit...

The best-kept secret in Network Marketing is that your long distance lines are your strongest ones.

Most people think it's just the opposite. They think that their local group is the strongest, because they have the most people there. They see more people, more often at the functions. And there seems to always be people coming by their house, picking up products or borrowing sales tools.

In actuality, your local line is often your most codependent line. You'll notice that people on a line 3,000 miles away don't call you when they need products; they don't call to see if you have an extra distributor kit they can borrow; and they don't ask you to do the presentation for their hot new prospect. They maintain enough inventory because they know there is no one there to cover for them. Because they are far away, they learn self-sufficiency.

Another benefit of working long distance is that it forces you to do what you should be doing anyway with your local lines—which is to work yourself out of a job.

Starting a new line...

Now, if you cannot get somewhere in three hours, then we're talking about a long distance line. Many times these lines will be in places where you need to get on a plane or train and drive many hours to get there. So here's the formula for working with those lines. I wouldn't recommend you sponsor anyone long distance unless you're willing to follow this procedure.

In my company, we have a business plan, which is a booklet that takes someone through their fast start training. I overnight the booklet to new people who are long distance and ask them to call me as soon as they've finished reading it. This takes them through the procedural training, their candidate list, etc. They've got to demonstrate that they have done the whole training, have their list ready, and are willing to go core.

Then I will help them via phone, email, and the weekly team leadership call to get started. I stress the importance of using third-party tools and make myself available for three-way calls when they have a prospect they can't get off the fence. I also encourage them to use the network of opportunity meetings we have around the world when they have a candidate in a city offering such a meeting.

Of course, they'll want to know how soon I will come and conduct an opportunity meeting or training for them. I'm happy and willing to do this, but only after they have done their homework. I want to see at least 15 or 20 core distributors, each doing their own Major Blast. Once that happens, there's enough critical mass going that if I fly in, they'll have a great turnout for the event and things can really start to take off.

You also want to give them benchmarks to reach by the time you return. Give them a stretch goal of a certain amount of attendance for their regular opportunity meetings and return when they reach it. Following this process will ensure that your travels to other markets are an investment, instead of an expense.

Long distance lines are even more powerful than the local lines, because they give you destinations to visit; they make you friends all over the country, and often the world; and they protect your income by diversifying it.

Chapter Fourteen:

Harnessing the Power
of the Internet

In the course of human history, probably nothing thus far has made a bigger impact on humankind then the Internet will. I believe it is bigger than the Agricultural Revolution, the Industrial Revolution, and the telephone, telegraph, and computer all put together. It is completely transforming three of the most important things in the world—the way we communicate, the way we buy products and services, and the way we learn and acquire information.

It's amazing how many parallels there are between Network Marketing and the Internet. Both were considered revolutions in the way business is done. Both are about educating the consumer. And both were pioneers in eliminating the middleman and empowering the consumer to buy direct from the manufacturer. So you have to figure when you combine the two mediums, amazing things will happen.

When I wrote earlier editions of this book, some of the technologies the Internet brought us were not widely adopted enough to be duplicable. But technology has advanced so fast and been so widely accepted that there are now lots of developments that can help you grow your business and be duplicated at the same time. Let's look at some of the ways you can do this:

Communication...

Email has become the method of choice for communicating with large groups of people. Even 90-year-old grandmas are emailing pix of their grandchildren today, so it duplicates well as a communication tool to stay in touch with your group. The number of people not on email is now so small it is negligible.

Most MLM companies maintain an email database and send regular announcements to their team. It's immediate, easy, and cheap.

Training...

We still do a weekly Leadership Training call for our team, but now it is streamed online at the same time. This allows people all over the world to log in without paying long distance charges. We also are doing a monthly product training webcast, conducted entirely online.

Like email, the technology has advanced so fast that duplication is no longer an issue. Bandwidth issues have been resolved, and online presentations are accessible to everyone around the world at the click of a mouse.

You can have open private rooms and host a guest chat on some sites. You can get your group together and let them ask questions of a high pin rank distributor. Use these rooms or the chat services to communicate with your overseas lines. Of course, SKYPE is also available, but personally I find their sound quality often lacking, and it seems to create interference on conference bridge lines. A service I'm using a lot these days is GoToMeeting.com.

We also have a very extensive website we maintain for our organization. It has training audios, videos, and PDF downloads of the business plan and other documents. We also use it to post the upcoming live training events and the worldwide network of opportunity meetings. We've just started streaming our meetings live around the world.

Before we leave training, you should know about www.NetworkMarketingTimes.com. This is a generic MLM site that sells my other training resources. I contribute articles as well as write the *MLM Success Blog* there. When you visit, be sure to subscribe to *The MLM Leadership Report,* my free email newsletter.

Prospecting...

Okay, here's where it gets dicey. The Internet offers some great opportunities to recruit. But there are several issues that are cause for concern.

Issue number one is the tidal wave of "MLM Morons" who are all over the Internet, Spamming people, posting obnoxious messages on every possible forum, chat room, and networking site, and just generally making a public nuisance of themselves.

The Internet is a great place to meet people and make new friends. And we know from earlier chapters that the best way to prospect is to meet people and make new friends. But there is a right way and a wrong way to do this. The same rules from the physical realm apply in the cyberspace realm.

If your strategy is to meet people in line at the

supermarket and immediately try to pitch them about your opportunity, you're not going to impress many people. It's no different if you assault someone you've just met in a chat room. You demonstrate no respect or concern for the other person, you have no manners, and you come across as desperate. (Which you obviously are.)

The way to be successful online is to approach your online relationships the same way you do your offline ones.

Go out and look to meet some new people. As you make new friends, add them to your prospect list. Then, when it's time to open a couple of new lines, go over your prospect list, select the best candidates, and approach them in a businesslike way.

You can discover the best places to meet people online just like you do offline. Go where you will find people with commonalities with you. AOL, Yahoo, and MSN all have communities or sub-groups of people with similar interests. You'll find groups from stamp collecting to car enthusiasts, from belly dancers to racquetball players. Join the communities that interest you.

Next, look for actual stand-alone sites that are devoted to your interests. Simply type a keyword search of your hobbies and you're likely to pull up dozens or even hundreds of sites. You probably have several that you already visit now. Look for the ones that have community features like chat rooms, news groups, and message posting boards. Then participate.

Offer information, start a dialogue, and just get to know people. You will develop some online relationships that can develop into deeper ones. Then just like offline, the time will come when it makes sense to approach your friends about your opportunity.

Web 2.0 and the social networking sites...

Probably the biggest explosion in the Internet is the advent of the user-generated content and social networking sites like MySpace, Facebook, and YouTube.

These sites are great ways to meet people as well. And like the other sites mentioned, you want to use them to find friends and develop relationships, not view them as a whole new universe of victims you can assault with prospecting messages.

Now here's the second serious issue I mentioned. People tend to view these online options as replacements for doing the fundamentals. The Internet does not replace meetings and face-to-face contact, and contrary to what you read, you can't build a huge group sitting at home in your robe and bunny slippers.

Approach these networking sites for what they are—a place for meeting people and developing relationships. Then as these relationships develop, you are naturally going to come across people who will want your products and opportunity. View these sites simply as another way to meet people and expand your warm market, not places to post links to your recruiting sites.

I sponsor several people a month as a result of the relationships I've developed online. Now the interesting thing is I don't even have a website that I use for this! And I have been the number one income earner in my company over the last two and a half years. There are people in my company who have spent thousands of dollars creating websites, and they earn a fraction of what I do. So I really don't think people need to build websites to be an MLM distributor.

Now, my company, like a lot of others, recently set up a master site with replicating versions for individual team members. If your company has this option, go ahead and use it. But if they don't, you can still work fine with your email account and perhaps a team site.

That is the one thing we did as a team that worked well for us. We posted a page with a short sizzle audio and a video recording of an opportunity meeting. When working with people long distance, we simply send them a link to that page and then follow up after they view it.

The key is keeping things simple and duplicable. Which leads us to the other danger you have to watch out for...

Last week we did a short training at one of our major events on how to use social networking sites to expand a warm market. I got a message from one of my Diamond Directors that since then he's been bombarded with messages from his team on where to host their site, how to set up autoresponders, the best way to set up a blog, and other questions like these.

We don't want them to use any of these. We recommend that they set up some profiles only on MySpace, Facebook, and maybe a few special sites in the area of their hobbies. The other site that is coming on strong as I write this is Twitter. It's essentially a micro-blog, where you post updates up to 140 characters. I find this site more geared to business, and people are open to business messages. But like the other sites, if you expect people to follow you, your postings should be interesting, offer value, and not be hammering them with obnoxious sales pitches.

When you do set up your social media presence, be sure and find me and make a friend request on Facebook and MySpace. Also look for the MLM Mastery group I host on Facebook. And you can follow me on Twitter at http://twitter.com/Randy_Gage.

Bottom line: The Internet can help you with communication and training to make you more productive. And it can be helpful in expanding your warm market. But if you're spending more than 20 minutes a day working your business online, it's probably too much.

Here's my rule on this: The time you're visiting online sites and groups for your hobbies and interests DOES NOT count toward your ten to 15 hours a week you need to build your business. Just like if you meet your friends for coffee to discuss comic books, Sci-Fi, or adventure racing. Now, if during your conversation with those friends they express a need, and you know your business can help them fulfill that need, you can go into help mode. But just as you would not count your coffee klatch time as work hours, don't count all the hours you spend surfing the Net and chatting people up as doing your business.

All told, the Internet is changing the way we do business. Prospecting, communication, and training will all become easier through the power of the Net. Just don't let it pull you off of the fundamentals.

Chapter Fifteen:

Developing Your Most Important Resource

Virtually every person in the world has the ability to create a massive network marketing organization. Yet most people never will.

Now, this would seem completely crazy. Because realistically, who wouldn't want to be their own boss, set their own hours, pick the people they work with, have unlimited income potential, and go to bed every night knowing that what they do empowers others?

So, why doesn't everyone do this?

I believe it's because they are not willing to do the necessary work on themselves that would allow them to accept success. Put another way—they won't let themselves become a successful person.

Even before I began this project, I knew that no how-to book on Network Marketing would be complete without addressing the issue of self-development. I've learned that how fast your organization grows is directly related to the speed at which you yourself grow.

Frankly, I don't know why this is or how it works. But I do know that this is exactly what happens. Your network will grow only as fast as you do. This was a lesson I learned the hard way.

I often joke with seminar audiences that I got into this business for three reasons:

1) To make money.
2) To make money.
3) To make money.

They laugh and I laugh, but that was no joke. I entered the business solely because I saw it as my only chance to get rich. And, thus, I began my career with a mercenary zeal to make lots of money. Every action I took was calculated to make me money. As a result, I made none.

I couldn't see it at the time, but my selfish, narrow-minded focus alienated people and actually *prevented* me from making money. What I got instead was a lot of frustration and rejection and an even lower bank balance—which, fortunately, ultimately led to a greater good.

My total lack of success humbled me and finally caused me to come to the conclusion that I could learn from others. Or, more importantly, that I had no other choice if I wanted to be successful in the business.

As a result, I made a conscious effort to befriend successful people in the business. I wanted to learn what the secret of building a business was—what they knew that I didn't. It was quite disconcerting at first...

It seemed that every leader I spoke with had a different way of doing the business. Some held meetings; some built by mail; others did only one-on-ones; and some concentrated mostly on retail.

It was only after extensive study that I learned that most of these people really couldn't put their finger on what caused them to be successful. More importantly, I came to the realization that they had achieved their own brand of success, but not the kind I was looking for.

These people had what I considered large incomes at the time, but none of them seemed to be retired or have true residual income. Most of them had nice bonus checks but were working ten to 14 hours a day. It was this revelation that made me understand the importance of true duplication and ultimately caused me to create my duplicable system.

But creating that system was not the primary reason for my success, nor the success of the people who follow my system...

Success in this business comes from something much deeper—something I learned from all of those leaders I had befriended. For although they all seemed to approach the business in a different way, I did discover a commonality that each of them possessed:

A passion for learning, self-development, and personal growth.

These people listened to audio programs, read books, and went to seminars. They spent a specific portion of each day on self-development. And it seemed that the more successful they were, the more time they spent working on themselves.

This was an amazing new concept for me. I had never been to a seminar in my life. I didn't even know they existed. I read mystery novels and political books, but I had no idea that there was such a category as self-help literature.

When I hung around those leaders, they all talked about books like *Think and Grow Rich, How to Win Friends and Influence People,* and *The Magic of Thinking Big.* They spoke of these in revered tones. These books were old friends they had visited with again and again. At last, I had found "the secret!"

This was the one thing that all leaders, with all different approaches, had in common.

This was something I could model, and my people could duplicate.

I learned that if there really were any secret to the business, it was this: If you want to reach a certain status, or certain goal, *you have to become the kind of person who would reach that status or that goal.* The talents are hidden within you, waiting to be unleashed. What you have to do is let them come forth.

You must eliminate all the negative and lack programming you've been exposed to, almost since birth, and get back to your natural essence. The doubts, fears, and uncertainties you have were learned. Now you must unlearn them.

Do you believe in universal laws?

If you're like most people, you do. You've come to believe that things are controlled by cause and effect, and you understand that gravity, centrifugal force, and other such laws are governed by immutable, unshakable principles. If you hit a baseball, it will project forward. If you throw an object in the air, it will fall back to earth. You must plant a seed and nurture it to grow a plant.

Next question...

Do you believe the same universal laws govern your own life and business? Now here's where it gets interesting. Most people believe these laws govern the entire universe, but things that happen in their own life are *coincidence, chance,* and *luck.*

Fascinating.

When they see someone else get hit by a car, they

think, *"Why didn't that dummy look where he was going?"* Yet if *they* fail to look before they step into the road and get hit by a car, they attribute it to "bad luck."

They believe the moon, stars, planet rotation, climates, nature, evolution, mathematics, and physics are all controlled by universal laws. But when they get fired, have dysfunctional relationships, develop addictions, or suffer bad business results, these things get explained as bad luck, coincidence, tough breaks, and other rationalizations—*all of which denote them as an innocent victim.*

Just how often are you a victim? And just how innocent are you, really?

It's a fascinating subject. The lament I hear most from people in the business is "I wish I could find more people like me." Unfortunately, their problem is actually quite the opposite. They *have* attracted people exactly like them.

I know this from firsthand experience. When I joined the business, I was very excited and leveraged that excitement to sponsor a few people. Then, when the excitement wore off, I stopped sponsoring and instead devoted my efforts to calling up my three or four people and encouraging them to make me rich.

For some reason, they didn't share my enthusiasm. I couldn't understand this at all. I felt I had done my part, since I had introduced them to the business and sponsored them in. Now I felt they weren't living up to their part of the bargain. They were supposed to duplicate this process and ensure *my* success. Then, it would be up to their downline people to take care of their success.

I felt as long as they recruited a few serious people like me who understood the system, duplication would be assured. These new people—if they were like me—would recognize that their job was to go with the program, reward their sponsor, and trust that they would receive their own reward in the end.

My whole strategy was based upon two elements: *fear* and *entitlement*.

The fear was my fear of rejection and fear of failure—both of which had prevented me from approaching anyone who was even moderately successful. Because of this, I had only approached people like me—fearful people who were easy targets for my message of getting rich quick.

I was naïve, gullible, and not even remotely aware of the principles on which success is founded. I thought Network Marketing was a shortcut to success, a way to cheat the system and get rich without having to do all the work.

My thinking was "I found this shortcut, and now I've shared it with you. Your job is to find other people to duplicate this and give me the reward due me for introducing it to you in the first place."

Unfortunately, because my whole approach was based around my own fears, I attracted people just like me—fearful. And although they were just like me, they didn't duplicate the same results. (If they would have, I still would have made money. Even though I would have had a fearful group, the growth would keep coming.)

What actually happened is they duplicated the actions they were seeing from me. Or more accurately, the lack of action.

I sponsored in the initial people and then went

into management mode. You know—trainings at my house, lots of calls, plenty of busywork, but no actual sponsoring. This is what was duplicated in my group.

My organization had the best briefcases, file systems, plastic page protectors, and training meetings in the company. Unfortunately, by the third month, there were only about 11 of us left. My bonus check was in the neighborhood of $18, and I was spending about $100 a month on meetings, fuel, and other expenses.

I whined and moaned about why I couldn't attract more people just like me. The truth was—I had. I had an organization full of scared people, doing busywork all day, afraid to talk to any credible prospects. I felt ripped off from my entitlement, and I bemoaned the unfairness of it all.

Ah yes, entitlement. It's a funny thing. I read something yesterday about entitlement—although I can't remember who said it—that went something like this: "Don't think the world owes you a living. It was here before you were."

All I knew at that point, however, was that things weren't working out and somebody was responsible. It never occurred that it could be me...

I thought perhaps the products were too expensive, my sponsor was too stupid or too lazy, or maybe I lived in a city where Network Marketing didn't resonate well with the local population.

I looked everywhere but in the mirror...

I went to training seminars where people talked about investing in your business and learning new skills, but I discounted them, figuring they were just trying to sell me books and audios.

I went to company functions where leaders spoke

of sponsoring activities and follow-up, but I discounted them, figuring they were holding back the real "secrets" because they just wanted to make money off of me.

I went to motivational programs on getting out of my comfort zone but sat in the back row on the aisle— so I could leave when they started all that "rah-rah" stuff I was too cool for.

I talked with the most successful people in my sponsorship line. They told me to read positive books, listen to audios, and use affirmations and visualizations every morning. I discounted them, because obviously they were under the influence of soymilk and tofu burgers.

I had it all figured out. The one thing I couldn't understand was why I always got so many bad breaks and why I didn't get more empathy and sympathy from all those "lucky" people who had more success than me. I assumed they must have forgotten what it was like to be broke.

Actually, it was just the opposite. Many of them had come from the lack and limitation that I was in, but they refused to let me drag them back into it. Since they correctly assumed that I was not open to change, they smiled sadly and acknowledged my poor "victim" state of affairs—then couldn't wait to get away from me, which just proved my conspiracy theory about them withholding the magic secrets of success from me.

As you've probably surmised, a transformation took place...

Which is why I can write this book today. I won't go into the drama of it all, since that would be (and became) a book all its own. Suffice it to say, my transformation involved a string of dysfunctional relationships, near bankruptcy, therapy, and a lot of setbacks before I finally got the clue that there was ONE person who was always at the scene of the crime.

When I changed ME, I changed my group, my company, and the world. Or so it seemed. All I know is that when I changed, so did my results. Whenever I grew as a person, I saw an even bigger growth in my business and my happiness.

I discovered that Network Marketing was not a shortcut to success. I realized that the corporate rat-eat-rat mentality was a fraud, and Network Marketing was the real way to build security. But that true security came when you worked hard, acted with integrity, and continually grew as a person.

What's the bottom line in all this?

Network Marketing is not the shortcut to success, because there isn't any shortcut. However, MLM is a vehicle that if you practice the principles of work, fairness, and giving value, you can reach extraordinary success and help lots of others reach that same success.

But it all begins with self-development—being willing to become the kind of person successful people are.

It's important that you work on self-development, because as you reach different levels of success in the business, the skills necessary to perform the business will change.

Richard Brooke, the president of Oxyfresh, was speaking at a program with me, and he said something that I thought was probably the most profound statement of the entire weekend. I'm paraphrasing him here, because I don't have the exact words, but in essence he described his company as a leadership factory disguised as a personal care products company.

That's what I mean when I say that personal development is the stealth ingredient of this business. A lot of people don't recognize or understand that personal growth is really the ultimate benefit they receive from Network Marketing.

Yes, the money is nice, the cars are nice, the trips and the friendships are nice, as are the status and camaraderie. But what really sets Network Marketing apart—makes it head and shoulders above any other business—is the personal growth factor. The leadership skills you develop are a tremendous part of that personal growth.

You'll also learn to develop management skills. You'll be managing a very large organization—in many cases, a million-dollar or *multi*-million-dollar company. Now, you won't have employees, you won't have much paperwork, and you won't have a lot of the traditional headaches that go with a multi-million-dollar business. But you will still have a hugely successful business that needs to be managed on a daily basis. And you can acquire the skills to make that job easier.

Keep in mind the following philosophy that has served me well over the years:

> *You don't manage people. You lead people and manage things.*

Probably the most important step you can take in building your business is to make and keep a commitment to set aside time every day for self-development. Now, if your company offers something like a book-of-the-month or CD-of-the-week, this would be the perfect program to plug into. It's better for you to work with the program that your sponsorship line has, if it's available, because you'll be able to create some synergy and mastermind with other people in the organization. If, however, your company or sponsorship line does not have one, it's critical that you set up your own. Here's how this worked with me:

I started with 15 minutes a day of self-development time. I recorded an audio for myself (which today has become a best seller) called *Secrets of a Dynamic Day*. It was designed to get me focused before I left the house. In fact, I believe your day is created before you ever leave the house in the morning. So, I listened to the audio and spent 15 minutes reviewing my goal card, thinking about where I was going and what I wanted to accomplish, remembering to whom I had given packets, thinking of new people I could get packets out to, and just generally organizing what I would like to do throughout the day.

Now, I have to tell you, it was really difficult for me to listen to that tape every morning. I was one of those people who always woke up at the last possible second, ran late everywhere I went, and was usually desperate to jump on the highway and make up time to get to where I was already supposed to be. I had to force myself to listen to that tape each morning to become focused.

It was very difficult at first, but after a few days, I could tell I had become more organized. I started to have more time, arrived places when I was supposed to, and got more things accomplished. When I saw what this was doing for my productivity, I went up to 30 minutes a day for self-development.

I would listen to that tape, and then meditate or pray or exercise or do something that promoted my self-development—in essence, nourish my mind, body, and spirit. What that did was double my income. I was so much more productive, had so much more self-confidence, and felt such a great sense of purpose that magical things started to happen.

What that did to my income, my relationships, my spirituality, and every other area of my life prompted me to increase it even further. Nowadays, I will often take an hour or more for self-development.

I don't answer the phone; I don't answer the door; I don't check my email. I do my 30-minute cardio workout, which also serves as prayer and meditation time. Then I do a little exercise, read my Daily Word, and possibly get in some stretching. The result is I don't interact with people until my consciousness is up at its peak level. At that point, an interesting thing happens.

As I go forth into the world, I attract people who have the same level of consciousness. Whereas, in the past, when I was a victim, I always attracted people with a victim mentality, now that I have a higher consciousness, I attract people who have a higher consciousness as well.

In essence, what I did with this self-development program was make myself over. I was not happy with the person I had become, so I worked on me every day—consistently and persistently. Just a little bit, to get a little bit better each day.

I figure it took me about two years, but I was a completely new person by that time. Then, from that point, I became a completely new person in another year. And from that point, I felt that within another six months, I had completely "made over" myself again. I have found that the personal growth starts to build exponentially, just like your network does.

As you grow personally, your network grows at the same time. If you learn to speak another language, it will improve your network. If you study yoga, it will help your business. If you take continuing education courses on mathematics or carpentry or basket weaving, it will help your business. Anything you do that gets you out of your comfort zone will make you a stronger, better person, and thus, you will have a stronger, better business.

I do my self-development time in the morning. You may like it at night, or you may like to split it. The morning works better for me, because it motivates me to go out and be productive each day. Do what works best for you.

It took me a while to learn that success doesn't come from changing the people in your organization, changing your sponsorship line, or changing your company.

Success comes from changing you.

Would you like to have a growing, dynamic, empowering organization? It's easy. Simply become a growing, dynamic, empowering individual!

Chapter Sixteen:

Putting It All Together

I'd like to share my thoughts on how you put all of these pieces together and go out to build a massive network—your personal multi-level money machine. But before I do that, I'd like to share something else—call it "What you *don't* want to do to be successful." It's very much a tongue-in-cheek article I wrote a few years back that was published back in the day in *Upline* magazine under the pseudonym Ydnar Egag.

I received more response from this article than anything I'd ever written up to that time. Astute readers figured out what the byline spelled backward, and they called, wrote, or faxed to express their appreciation and amusement. That article has since been reprinted in at least five or six other trade publications.

Sad to say, some readers accepted it as gospel. They are so tied to the MLM-junkie, look-for-the-next-hot-deal syndrome, that they simply don't know there's another way. They've spent so long *getting ready to get ready* that they've lost touch with what building a network actually entails.

So, before we look at creating your action plan, here's my gift to you:

The Lazy Man's Guide to MLM Success

Stop working so hard. You're training your group, following through, going to meetings, investing a lot of time in new distributor orientations, etc. Don't you realize that you could be spending that time, instead, in your very own home, sipping a cold drink, and watching The Simpsons?

If you wanted to work, you would have stayed with your regular job. The reason you got into networking was to kick back and let other people make you rich. So, let's look at the proper way to do that:

First of all, you want to choose the right companies. Now, it's hard to stay focused, so you definitely don't want to have more than, say, 15. A lot of the best HOT companies have a habit of closing up, so if you don't have some spare ones, you will lose credibility with your downline.

Look for companies you can build by just mailing postcards or tapes to multi-level junkies. They already know how to mail postcards to other MLM junkies, so you won't have to waste any time training them.

Avoid any companies that have anything to do with selling products, buying products, or holding meetings. If you must buy products, try to find a company where you can buy your way into the car fund, directorship, etc. You can always unload the stuff on your new distributors. Any companies over six months old are already over the hill, so avoid them like the plague. Try to find "no-brainers" where they build your downline for you.

Another pitfall to avoid is companies with beautiful four-color literature. That stuff costs a fortune! Find a company that uses economical Xerox copies and tenth-generation videotapes.

Try to find corporate leaders who have bounced around from one company to another, and who've been shut down by the attorney general once or twice. These are the seasoned pros who know their way around. They learned from the school of hard knocks—so you don't have to.

*Once you have this portfolio of companies selected, it's time to begin the **analyzation stage**.*

This is a critical time for your business, so don't rush it. Basically, what you want to do here is review every single piece of literature from every single program. Then, watch all the videos, listen to all the audios, and go to any trainings. Read all the "Big Al" books and everything from Tim Sales and Randy Gage.

Now that you're well versed in the industry, start analyzing your marketing plan. Compute all the percentages to make sure that the company didn't make any errors. Then, figure out how much money you're going to make with 10,000 people in your downline. Do the same thing with 20,000, 30,000, and so forth up to a million. Now, you figure a plan to accomplish this.

Example:

You will mail out 100 postcards. Seventy-five people will join your program. They will each mail out 100 postcards the next month after which 75 will join, so you will have 5,700 distributors by the end of the second month. In the third month, they repeat the process, so you will have 40,000, and so on and so on. Now compute your volume if they all buy just $30 worth of products. Now, figure with $50, then $75, and so on. Deduct a small percentage for the deadbeats who don't want to work, and you can get an accurate picture of your income. Call your sponsor and see if he has sponsored anybody under you yet.

After you have properly analyzed,

pontificated, and meditated for at least three months, it's time to move on to the **preparation stage.**

First of all, go out and rent the biggest office you can find. Rent some swanky office furniture as well. Try to find the same desk and chair that Blake Carrington used in Dynasty. *You want to show people you're serious about success. Don't get nervous about the costs—remember those income projections you've got on paper.*

If your spouse is giving you a hard time, explain that this is not "another one of those deals." This is different. Anyway you'll close his or her trap when you pull up in your new Bentley.

Put up some diplomas, degrees, plaques, and other status indicators around the office. Let people know that networking is not for the average slob—you need to be an experienced professional like yourself. Besides, it's nice when your downline has the proper hero worship for you.

Another important step in the preparation process is **Starter Kit Preservation.** *NEVER OVERLOOK THIS STEP!!!*

Get some Avery brand (don't settle for cheap

imitations) white reinforcements, and put one on the front and one on the back of each hole of each page in your binder. Make sure that you don't miss any or the page could come loose, and then what would you do?

After the reinforcements are applied, enclose every single page of the kit in plastic page protectors. Otherwise you never know when a careless slip from somebody's coffee cup could bring your networking career to a screeching halt!

Once your starter kit is protected, you can begin printing stationery, business cards, postcards, etc. Buy a new briefcase, appointment book, electric pencil sharpener, and get yourself a new wardrobe. Get a large file cabinet and stapler, and buy a computer system for doing your newsletter. You don't want people to see you driving that old beater, so rent a Lexus to tide you over until your company bonus car comes in. If all of this is taxing your spouse's take-home pay, just tap those credit cards. Remember, "Fake it until you make it."

Next, you want to study your sponsor's presentation and find the weaknesses. Create your own special, unique presentation that can be changed weekly. Also, develop some audios, brochures, and flipcharts on your own. These are always better than the company's, and it allows you to exercise your creative abilities. It's important that you set this example. You want leaders, not sheep!

After these first stages are completed, only then are you ready to talk to anyone about your business! If you tried to sponsor anyone before this four- to six-month process was completed, they might have asked a question you couldn't answer, and you would have lost credibility.

Unfortunately, by the time you've reached this stage, probably several of your companies have closed down. But don't worry, that's what the spares are for.

*You are now ready for the **Postcards to Strangers Stage.** Don't talk to your friends, neighbors, or relatives. They're all skeptics and losers! Besides, think how much time it would take to train them. Let them see how much money you'll be making in a couple of months, and they'll come crawling to you, begging to join. Just get yourself a list of fully trained, serious MLM junkies and mail out those 100 postcards!*

*Once your 75 distributors sign up, you can move into the **Hot Bath Hype Stage.***

Since these lightweights don't understand the big picture like you do, it's important to keep them motivated. Get some copies of big checks from the heavy hitters and wave them under their noses.

The biggest problem you will face is that most of these people are sluggards and procrastinators. They want to analyze everything to death when they should be out making you money. They think money grows on trees; they don't realize that it has to be earned.

Call them daily and check up to see if they've sponsored anybody. Let them know that if they want to make the big bucks, they'd better get off their butt. At the end of the month, call everybody and remind them to order or you won't get a check. Let them know that if they don't toe the line, you've got a new distributor just a postage stamp away.

If the majority of your people aren't producing, it can mean one of two things. Your programs have all peaked and are over the hill, or these just weren't hot programs worthy of somebody of your caliber. Either way, it's time to chuck those turkeys and start looking for the next HOT deal. Let the losers work those programs that take time, money, and commitment—a heavy hitter like you has no need of such things. Just get out there and get RICH!!

****

Don't you wish it were that easy? Well, the truth is, this business is not all that difficult either. It's not easy, but it is simple.

If you have a big dream, you're coachable, and you're willing to put in ten to 15 hours a week, you really can become successful in Network Marketing.

You can be a Ph.D. or a high school dropout like me. You can have a healthy war chest, or you may have to borrow the money to get started, as I did.

You can analyze your compensation plan and you can research the profession and perform a due diligence on your company; but, ultimately, those things won't mean as much as who you are and what you do.

Believe it or not, your company, and even the profession, is not the opportunity. You are. Your company and Network Marketing are simply the vehicles that allow you to express your own inherent talent.

You are the opportunity, but you have to take the necessary steps to manifest it. It's very easy to fall into the procrastination and analyzing trap. Most of us have a lot of negative programming that lets us easily fall prey to such thinking. The reality is that Network Marketing has proven itself to be a viable business entity, a state-of-the-art distribution system, and an empowering vehicle for personal growth and lifestyle fulfillment.

The new cars paid for, the dream houses built, and

the millionaires created are simply too numerous to calculate.

More importantly, how many relationships were strengthened or saved because spouses came together to work toward a common goal? How many mothers (and fathers) got to go back home and raise their own kids, instead of paying someone else to do it?

How many millions of people—who have never even been a distributor—have had their lives enhanced because of products supplied by a network marketing company? What about the pounds lost, the nutritional deficiencies alleviated, the energy restored, or maybe just the money saved on the monthly phone bill that was put to better use?

How many more people support charities because of the money and freedom they've earned from Network Marketing? A future president, the doctor who finds a cure for a disease, or the person who creates the starship that can take us to Jupiter may be the person who got a college education on the money their parents are earning today in Network Marketing.

Yes, there are tens of thousands of people who are in the business but will never get rich with Network Marketing. I'm okay with that. Because the potential is there for them. It is their choice whether or not to accept it. If they find products that enhance their lives, if they develop a sense of community with positive, goal-setting, dream-building people, then their lives are better than when they joined.

Most people will benefit from the products; some will benefit from the personal growth; and the serious ones will become wealthy. I'm hoping that you will do all three. That's why I wrote this book. To share and give back, in the best way I know how, for all of the many blessings I've received.

You can really build a massive, empowering, and exponentially growing organization if you follow the specific steps I've outlined here. Network Marketing and the systems I teach are not unknown commodities. They work. Everywhere.

I've done "Get Started" meetings in Skopje, Macedonia, conducted Leadership Institutes in Zagreb, Croatia, given training seminars in Sydney, Australia, and held opportunity meetings in Ljubliana, Slovenia. Thousands have done it. Millions more are doing it.

The principles are the same everywhere. They transcend cultures, economic situations, and even time. The power of a dream is the most awesome force that humankind can harness. Electrical generators, nuclear power plants, even the atomic bomb are minuscule by comparison. The only obstacles that can stop you are the ones you see in the mirror every morning.

What it is going to take is making three investments in yourself...

First, invest in a commitment. A commitment that you really are worthy of success and that you'll do whatever it takes to achieve it.

Second, invest your time. Of course, it's not easy to find ten to 15 hours a week. If it were, everybody would be doing it. But if you tell yourself, "I'll do it after school's out" or "I'll have time after the holidays," you're in denial, lying to yourself. If you really believe you're worthy, you'll act NOW.

I know that finding the time involves sacrifice. But making a sacrifice for two to four years—in exchange for a lifetime of freedom—is a pretty good investment in my book.

Do me a favor—don't ever use your kids as an excuse not to do the business. Use them as the *reason* to do the business. It would be worth missing one more evening a week with them for two years to then be with them every day and make all the PTA meetings, school plays, soccer matches, and little league games after that.

And please. Don't use your spirituality as an excuse not to do the business. I must tell you. I missed some nights in church and some Sundays too, when I was on the road working long distance. I held my own service. Because, in my faith, we believe that there's nothing spiritual about being poor. In fact, we teach that being poor is a sin. I believe that your Creator wants you to be healthy, happy, and prosperous. It is your birthright.

I have prosperity now because I made choices along the way. And you know what? I serve on my church's committees; I've been the president of the board of trustees; and I tithe more than most people make. Because I didn't use my spiritual identity as an excuse for inaction, but rather, as a reason for action.

Third, invest your money. I don't think you'll find a more disproportionate reward or return on an investment in any business today than what's possible with Network Marketing. But you still have to invest something.

You need business-building materials; you need self-development materials; and you have to attend functions. If you don't have enough money, sell your television! You'll probably be better off without it anyway. If you don't invest in you, who will?

Another thought on investment. Please don't live out of your business if you want a big business. Keep your day job in the beginning—as distasteful as that sounds—so you can reinvest everything you make back into your business. Like everything else, a little sacrifice early will pay much greater rewards down the road. Network Marketing works on the principle of delayed gratification. Invest in yourself for two to four years, and then reap the rewards for a lifetime.

As your income builds, learn to manage your money so you can create real wealth. There are a lot of people in Network Marketing who have earned millions of dollars and are broke anyway. Pay your taxes, invest in the future, and learn how to grow your net worth.

Finally, set the example for your group. Work hard; support your people; use the products; and have fun! Model integrity and a work ethic that your group can duplicate. Because you know what? They will!

As you approach any decision in your business, ask yourself this simple question: Will this bring me closer to my dream or take me further away from it?

You must be willing to pay the price—and that means taking action. Each day, you must make consistent, persistent, positive movement toward your dream. If you keep information packets in circulation; practice self-development; attend the functions; and are teachable, you really will live your dreams.

I didn't write this book to challenge your dreams, but rather to help you realize them. And I certainly didn't write it to change you but to share with you what I have learned so you might discover and unfold who you really are. Relish the journey, my friend. You're about to take a magic carpet ride of challenge, adventure, and growth.

Enjoy the ride!

-RG

About the Author

There is probably no one on earth better qualified to help you reach more success in MLM than **Randy Gage**. His Duplication Nation (formerly How to Earn at Least $100,000 a Year in Network Marketing) is the top selling training album in MLM, and his Escape the Rat Race is the #1 recruiting tool in the business. His resources have been translated into more than 15 languages and sold in the millions around the globe.

Randy helped introduce Network Marketing in places like Slovenia, Croatia, Bulgaria and Macedonia. He's been a company VP of Marketing, and served as a consultant to numerous companies, designing compensation plans, creating marketing materials and developing duplicable systems for them. Randy has conducted training for the finest companies in the industry, and spoken in more than 35 countries.

Through his coaching programs and private consulting, Randy has helped the top income earners in numerous companies. He has arguably trained more MLM millionaires than anyone alive today. But most importantly, Randy teaches from real-world experience, earning millions of dollars as a distributor.

Randy has conducted thousands of training programs and presented thousands more opportunity meetings. Several years ago he dusted off his white board and starting from scratch he quickly rose to become the #1 income earner in his company worldwide. He knows what is working in the marketplace right now, and he'll teach you exactly how to reach mega success in these conditions.

Randy has made his money, and continues to work only for the challenge and to support his personal enrollees. He has achieved the perfect balance between work and life. When he's not drawing circles, you'll find him playing 3rd base for the South Florida Carnivores, riding his bike, racing cars, or collecting comic books. His guilty pleasures are Sci-Fi, Krispy Kreme, and watching Project Runway. Randy splits his time between Miami Beach, Sydney, and Paris.

www.RandyGage.com

Additional Information

How to Build A Multi-Level Money Machine:
The Science of Network Marketing
4th edition
by Randy Gage

Available directly from your local bookstore, online at
www.NetworkMarketingTimes.com, or you may also
contact us at:

Prime Concepts Group, Inc.
7570 W. 21st Street N., Suite 1038A
Wichita, KS 67205 USA

Toll-Free: 1-800-432-4243
Voice: (316) 942-1111
Fax: (316) 942-5313

To receive a free catalog featuring other quality network
marketing and self-development resources, visit us
online at www.NetworkMarketingTimes.com.

Recruit Better, Build Volume and Earn More!

www.NetworkMarketingTimes.com

NetworkMarketingTimes.com is the ultimate resource for generic MLM training tools, and prosperity and success resources. We are dedicated to helping those in the MLM, Network Marketing and Direct Selling profession to recruit faster, keep their representatives longer, and build long-term residual income. Network Marketing Times is a division of Prime Concepts Group, Inc., and the exclusive publisher and producer of Randy Gage MLM training and success tools.

The Ultimate Step-by-Step MLM System for Building Your Business

Available Formats: DVD, Audio CD or MP3 Download

Duplication Nation: How to Build a Massive Network Marketing / Direct Selling Organization

This is the most advanced training on the science of building an organization that has ever been offered.

It is a complete step-by-step system to growing an organization. It can help the industry beginner all the way to the seasoned professional.

Includes 12 audio CDs or 12 video DVDs, study guide and bonus business building materials.

Visit <u>www.NetworkMarketingTimes.com</u>

Making the First Circle Work

Available Formats:
Paperbak & eBook

The foundation for duplication in network marketing.

This powerful little book from Randy Gage is exactly what you need to get duplication really happening all the way through your organization.

Randy shows you the difference between what you really control and what you can only influence. Then you'll learn how to create the culture that causes true duplication.

**Visit <u>www.NetworkMarketingTimes.com</u>
to order your paperback or ebook today.**

Quantity discounts available.

Train Your New Distributors and Build Your Business

Fast Track Pack: Getting Started Training to Ensure Success in Network Marketing

Probably the most important component in your system is the training you give your new distributors is in the first 48 hours. These MLM training tools are the collateral support resources to train your new distributors on how to be a "business" person. They are the new distributor training tools Randy Gage recommends you use to train your people and stop distributor dropout!

This Set Includes:

- What You Need to Know First CD
- Getting Started CD
- Secrets of a Dynamic Day CD
- First Steps booklet
- Check Out the Biz DVD

Visit <u>www.NetworkMarketingTimes.com</u>

How to Become an
MLM Rock Star!

5 Audio CDs

Available Formats: Audio CD Album or MP3 Download

Duplication Strategies for Building
a Massive Network

This is the true "Insider" info that Randy used to build one of the fastest growing organizations ever seen in the industry.

This is NOT a training album on how to get a prospect's phone number, or product retailing tips! This is the high level, leadership and culture stuff, the information you need to lead a massive organization and guide it through exponential growth.

ATTN: This album is not for people who are just getting started in MLM / Network Marketing. We recommend that you begin your training with Randy's "Duplication Nation" album until you reach the need for higher levels of training before you purchase this album.

Visit <u>www.NetworkMarketingTimes.com</u>

Mega-MLM

Available Formats: Audio CD or Digital Download

There has NEVER been a more advanced, intense, high-level, breakthrough training on the profession of Network Marketing. EVER.

Recently a group of top-level achievers from around the world gathered for a very special and exclusive event. Now you can experience the exact training the live attendees did, in a Home Study version. It was recorded live and unedited, as it took place. You'll get the same handouts and a follow along workbook to help you reach the very highest levels of success in the profession.

Includes 11 audio CDs, study guide and bonus disc.

This is for the advanced network marketer; if you are just beginning we recommend that you begin with Randy Gage's "Duplication Nation" album.

To order visit <u>www.NetworkMarketingTimes.com</u>

Risky is the New Safe

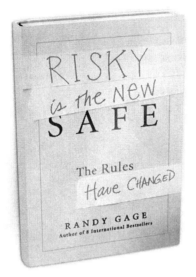

This is the textbook on getting rich!

This is a different kind of book for a different kind of thinking. It's a thought provoking manifesto for risk takers. Disruptive technology, accelerating speed of change and economic upheaval are changing the game. The same tired, old controversial thinking won't get you to success today.

Risky is the New Safe will change the way you look at everything!

Visit www.NetworkMarketingTimes.com

Quantity discounts available.

Secrets of Network Marketing
Volume 1

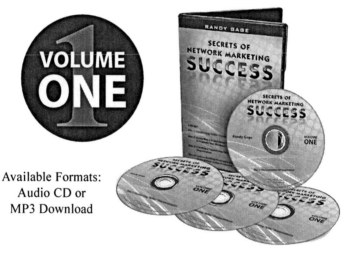

Available Formats:
Audio CD or
MP3 Download

Create powerful duplication in your Network Marketing organization.

Get the latest information on what's working today in the new economy. This is a "must have" resource for anyone that is serious about MLM success.

Volume One – 4-CD Set

- Disc 1: The Foundation for Duplication
- Disc 2: Using the Web and Social Networking to Explode Your Business
- Disc 3: Creating a "Leadership Factory" in Your Organization
- Disc 4: Culture Building Strategies of the Multi-Million-Dollar Producers

To order *Volume 1* and other volumes visit:
www.NetworkMarketingTimes.com

Secrets of Network Marketing
Volume 2

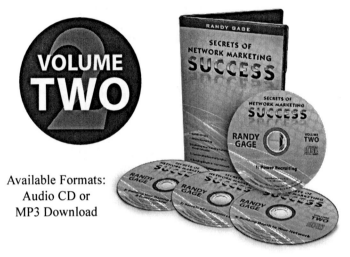

Available Formats:
Audio CD or
MP3 Download

This dynamic new resource is just what you need to explode your network marketing business!

In Volume One you learned how to grow a strong team. Now in this follow up resource you'll discover how to get duplication into play so your bonus check can multiply!

Volume Two – **4-CD Set**

- Disc 1: Power Recruiting
- Disc 2: Building Your Training Culture &
  Event Calendar
- Disc 3: Secrets of Influential Leaders
- Disc 4: Building Depth in Your Network

**To order *Volume 2* and other volumes visit:
www.NetworkMarketingTimes.com**

Check Out the Biz

Available Formats:
DVD or VHS

Build residual income & create financial security!

Check Out the Biz was filmed live before an audience of more than 1,000 people, so it offers an exciting and compelling presentation for your prospects. Use it to speed up your sponsoring and duplication rates. Randy knows how to grab the prospect's attention, and really drive home why they'd be crazy not to build a business.

Your prospects will learn:

- The benefits of owning their own MLM business;
- Why MLM is the new paradigm in distribution;
- How the industry will be expanding in the next few years; and,
- Why they should get involved now!

Visit <u>www.NetworkMarketingTimes.com</u> to order.

Quantity discounts available.

Lifestyle Freedom Pack

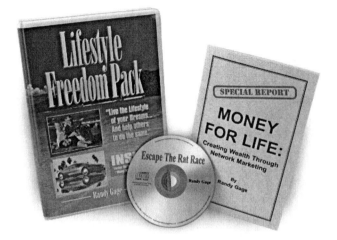

Stop getting rejected!

The hardest part of networking for most people is facing rejection from their friends and family. Here's how you can remove rejection from your sponsoring process.

Use the Lifestyle Freedom Pack to screen out non-prospects and qualify the real ones. Basically, this is an opportunity meeting in an album! It helps you sponsor faster, and duplicate easier.

The Freedom Pack contains the Escape the Rat Race CD and the Money for Life Special Report.

Visit <u>www.NetworkMarketingTimes.com</u> to order.

Quantity discounts available.

Discover how to build your volume, recruit more leaders and earn the BIG bonus checks

FREE Six-Week MLM-Mastery e-Course

MLM Legend Randy Gage reveals the insider secrets that can make you the next MLM Millionaire! Take the course that makes you a MLM Master! This powerful e-Course will be delivered free to your in-box each week for six lessons. You will learn how to build a huge network with strong duplication and lucrative passive income.

- Week 1: What You Need to Succeed in the Business
- Week 2: The Foundation for Rapid Duplication
- Week 3: Recruiting the Best Prospects
- Week 4: How to Create Exponential Growth
- Week 5: How to Develop Leaders in Your Team
- Week 6: Putting It All Together

Sign up for the *FREE* six-week MLM-Master e-Course at <u>www.NetworkMarketingTimes.com</u>

Connect with Randy Gage

www.RandyGage.com

www.NetworkMarketingTimes.com
Your Online Source to Help You Recruit Better,
Build Volume and Earn More

Like Randy
www.facebook.com/randygage

Follow Randy
www.twitter.com/Randy_Gage

Subscribe to Randy
www.youtube.com/randygage

Join Randy
www.linkedin.com/in/randygage

Join Randy's Circle
www.gplus.to/randygage

Connect with Randy
www.randygage.tumblr.com